Campfire
Tales GREAT LAKES

Campfire
Tales

GREAT LAKES

Schiffer
Publishing Ltd

4880 Lower Valley Road • Atglen, PA 19310

Skeletons from the watery depths and darkness below, fathoms beneath the shallow freedom of air we live upon, beckoning us to visit — to free them once more.

INTRODUCTION

Spooky Tales Around the Great Lakes

Everyone likes a good story. In my opinion, everyone *needs* a good story now and then. It's something we've done for eons—sharing tales with others is as old as humanity. I have so many fond memories of sitting around a late night campfire, roasting marshmallows until golden brown, eating crunchy, chocolaty, sticky s'mores—and hearing spooky ghost stories. Then, while safely snuggled in my sleeping bag, vivid images of the hauntingly good tales running rapid through my mind as the lights go out, making for an electrified and vigilant night—all the while waiting for the monsters to arrive.

The best tales told are ones in which you lose yourself—if only for a moment—tossed into a different world filled with mystery and strangeness, a landscape unknown. As the words are spoken, your eyes grow wide, your pulse surges, matching the rhythm of your racing heartbeat. You become one with the main character, wondering and wandering and hoping to live their adventure as if it were your own.

Campfire tales are always exciting to hear, but what would make them even better? How about if they were based on the truth? These kinds of stories are my favorite, which is why I enjoy writing them so much. And that is what you will get from the stories in this book. We have nearly a dozen stories collected, all focused on the myths and legends in and around the Great Lakes.

(By the way, how many of you know the Great Lakes by name? Do you know how many there are? Here's a clue: just remember the pneumonic H.O.M.E.S. That's **H**uron, **O**ntario, **M**ichigan, **E**rie, and **S**uperior. Now you'll never forget them. Of course, after reading the nightmarish tales covered in this book, you may try harder to forget.)

One begs to question why there are so many stories of ghosts and monsters near the Great Lakes. What makes it so alluring to the paranormal and all those supernatural beasts? There are many authorities on ghost hunting who indicate water has a great attraction for the spirits of the netherworld—a catalyst of energy. They can more easily appear, entering our world, if only for a moment. This phenomenon occurs along rivers as well, such as the Mississippi, or along other lakes and coastal waters. As for the Midwest, what better body of water for enticing spirits than the Great Lakes?

Recent map of the Great Lakes and surrounding area.

Before we get too far into the tales, myths, and legends, here are some interesting facts about the Great Lakes:

- **Huron:** The second largest of the Great Lakes, Huron has a surface area of 23,000 square miles—the third-largest fresh water lake on Earth. The maximum depth is 750 feet and it is 206 miles long and 183 miles wide at its greatest breadth. There are 3,827 miles of shoreline.

- **Ontario:** Lake Ontario is the smallest Great Lake in surface area, with 7,340 square miles and it is the fourteenth largest lake in the world. Its shoreline (including islands) is 712 miles. The maximum length is 193 miles and maximum width is 53 miles. The deepest part of the lake is 802 feet.

- **Michigan:** This is the only one of the five Great Lakes located entirely within the United States. It's the second largest by volume and third largest by surface area: 22,300 square miles. Michigan's maximum depth is 923 feet, and it is 307 miles long by 118 miles wide. It has 1,638 miles of shoreline.

- **Erie:** The fourth largest of the Great Lakes and tenth largest in the world, this lake is named after the Erie tribe of Native Americans who lived along its southern shore. The maximum depth is 210 feet (the shallowest), and its 241 miles long and 57 miles wide. It has 871 miles of shoreline.

- **Superior:** The largest of the Great Lakes, this water body is considered to be the largest freshwater lake on earth by surface area, which is 31,700 square miles. Its maximum depth is 1,332 feet and it is 350 miles long and 160 miles wide. Superior has 2,726 miles of shoreline.

As you can see, there is a lot of fresh-water locked up in the Great Lakes—twenty-one percent of the world's surface fresh water to be exact. Together, their surface area is a whopping 94,250 square miles and is sometimes referred to as America's "Third Coast." With such a large concentrated body of water, it's no wonder so many spirits and supernatural forces appear.

So, are you curious about which kinds of spirits are festering among the Great Lakes? Well, there are ghosts in Duluth, Minnesota, haunting the Glensheen Mansion, which is situated right off the north shore of Lake Superior. But then that's typically what you'll get when innocent and defenseless people are murdered. It's ripe for a haunting.

Perhaps you are not too excited about ghosts. Then you may enjoy the tale about the water gods called Manitous—Native American spirits that live at the bottom of the lake, always looking for unsuspecting prey who dare to voyage across their domain. Such are the claims from those living and working around the Great Lakes. In particular, the "real" tale of the SS *Edmund Fitzgerald,* also known as the *"Mighty Fitz,"* sank in the deep waters of Lake Superior.

Then there's the myth about a giant moose, terrorizing innocent tourists off the North Shore of Lake Superior. The tale has a moose twice the size of any human and easily able to swallow you whole. What might make a moose grow so large? Maybe it's the water...

Of course we can't forget the classic tale of the Michigan Dogman—a creature that is half-man half-dog...or was it half-dog half-man? Either way, the story within will have you howling for more.

My personal favorite is the story of Melon Head Creatures living in a dark and forbidden forest off Lake Michigan. These creatures are the result of a mad scientist and an even madder gang of children with whom he had experimented. A wicked story indeed. I suggest you read it with the lights on.

Still not enough for you? How about giant turtles off Mackinac Island? Yes, you heard me; there's a giant, man-eating turtle of a tale based on ancient Native American myths. And did I mention Mackinac Island is a sacred burial ground with thousands of unmarked graves?

We have Storm Hags from Lake Erie, too, which are like the Manitous water gods, only a whole lot more evil and smelly. These watery witches are bent on snatching the souls of those sailing too close to her underwater world. Lake Erie has its share of shipwrecks, including the mysterious disappearance of the *Clevco*, a ship supposedly brought down by a monstrous Storm Hag.

Many of you perhaps have heard about the short dwarf-like creature known as the Red Devil of Detroit, who also goes by the name of Nain Rouge. Like you would suspect, the Red Devil is not something you smile and greet in a friendly manor—you run away as fast as you can...or your life will meet an early demise.

The book would not be complete if we didn't mention the Maiden of the Mist of Niagara Falls, off the Niagara River between Lake Erie and Lake Ontario. This old Native American tale is revisited, with two unwise and rambunctious young men meeting up with the maiden and having a not-so-pleasant ending.

How about a classic Lady in White tale? In this case, we have the White Lady of Ontario, with her sad, tragic, and early death, and now she hopes the same for you. If you run into her in or around Durand Eastman Park near Rochester, New York, you will know her fury and hope for a swift and painless death.

Hopefully, these tales will be an exciting and spooky read for you. What may make them even more interesting is the history section after each story, allowing you to see in greater depth what the actual events or myths were. Like I've mentioned, while these may seem to be a few good campfire tales, they are more than that: they are based on the real deal, which to me makes the story all the more exciting. And if you ever visit one of the locations, don't be surprised if something supernatural leaps out at you or wakes you in the dead of night.

When doing the research for this book, with all the supernatural occurrences reported, I couldn't help but think about some of my own strange happenings around the Great Lakes. Okay, maybe nothing seriously supernatural, but nonetheless it got me thinking. For instance, when fishing on Lake Michigan, I was amazed at its vastness. The wind that day didn't help, creating over five-foot swells and made most of us seasick, or lakesick if you will. We went several miles out to focus on the bigger fish, and the captain said the depth was over 800 feet. I couldn't fathom that much fresh water beneath us. And I wondered in amazement about the creatures that might be lurking below. There's lots of room for mischief and mayhem, in my opinion.

I thought about how quickly weather changes in the region. While staying at a cabin off Lake Superior, in January mind you, we often went to sleep with the crashing waves just beyond the cabin, only to wake with the silence of ice. The shoreline would frequently freeze up overnight, bringing an eerily subdued, morning landscape. Of course, I also couldn't forget my friend one night deciding to go swimming in the frigid waters of Lake Superior. He only made it a few seconds, then hopped out and ran straight for the shower. (Unfortunately, he ran into the wrong cabin. Our neighbors were not amused.)

Then there's the expedition I had to Two Harbors, Minnesota, searching for Bigfoot. I recruited my older brother and we spent the weekend searching the forest for the hairy creature. We even baited the beast with tropical fruit, figuring he'd love the change of taste, compared to nuts and berries and people he typically ate. (By the way, you can read about my Bigfoot adventures and other creatures in my previous book, *Strange Minnesota Monsters.*)

And in my many camping trips, I've often wondered about running into a giant moose. I mean, how big can they actually get? I've camped in Canada several times, driving through the back roads late at night, which really freaked me out. The last thing I wanted was to come around the corner and be confronted with a monster moose lumbering in the road. Or when I've been camping in the Boundary Waters Canoe Area (BWCA), I wondered if a stray moose might drop by, tearing through my tent, and looking for a midnight snack—such as me.

I suppose that's the truth about the excitement in these stories: always wondering about the unknown and how it may affect you. At least that's the way I look at it. With our heavily technical and all-plugged-in society, there's something to be said about the lack of mystery and the unknown. Nowadays we are just a Google search away from most answers.

Or maybe the unknown is just that much harder to find? I think it's a travesty we can't more readily explore the unknown. Today, we tend to fall into too many routines—into the world of the mundane and monotonous. Maybe it's time we take the challenge—break from the redundant domain of normalcy and live for the moment of unfamiliarity. Why not grasp the bull by the horns? Or maybe the moose by the antlers? Or the ghost by its...well, it's kind of hard to grab a ghost. Regardless, I hope you enjoy these stories and the history behind them. Maybe it will get you off the couch to do some investigating yourself. Just be careful. You may find what you're looking for...and some things you'd rather forget.

A ship in turmoil, similar in fate of the Mighty Fitz,
battling the waves and demons of the deep from
the depths of Lake Superior.

CHAPTER 2

The Other Legend of the *Edmund Fitzgerald*

The following entries are from a journal found in July of 1994 at the bottom of Lake Superior among the wreckage of the *Edmund Fitzgerald*.

Journal Entry: November 9, 1975, 2:15 p.m.

Yet another voyage for the *Fitz*, like so many other wintery expeditions: clear and sunny with a frosty November chill consuming all things living. The waves ebb and flow across the vastness of Lake Superior, consistent and easily manageable— like so many other trips. Yet somehow…this one seems different. Must be cautious. My sixth sense urges me to be on call. No, this voyage is not just different—the trip reeks of danger and peril. Regardless, I need the money and must trudge onward.

There should be no concern of course. After all, this is not the maiden voyage of the *Edmund Fitzgerald* that had occurred years ago, in June of '58 if I recall. No, I am confident the big *Fitz* will take care of us; I'm sure of it. If anything, it's nice to know I'm in the largest boat on the Great Lakes—the largest on fresh water in the world.

The ship has spent many years hauling taconite across the Great Lakes, mostly between Duluth and Detroit, never once skipping a beat. Setting many records for speed and capacity I might add—all the while with me on deck. I'm proud of her, of the other crew members as well. I just wish I could shake this horrible feeling churning in my stomach, like a rotten pasty. I need to concentrate on my duties as watchman, to keep an eye on the ship and everything in it. However, I can't help but to brood heavily on the threatening waves and wind. Were they getting bigger? Stronger? It shouldn't matter. The big *Fitz* will take care of us. It will easily traverse the waves of the Great Lakes. Yet something feels wrong…

Journal Entry: November 9, 1975, 4:05 p.m.

Something isn't right. That ugly feeling inside me is getting worse. I can't seem to quiet the fear pounding in my head. The weather isn't helping. Some sailors have a trick knee that warns them of any drastic change in the climate. For me, it's the knuckle on my middle finger. Normally I can make a fist like anyone else. But in times of bad weather, my fist will barely close, not without a great deal of pain. As is the case for me now. Although I do have to chuckle, as when I try to close my hand the middle finger stays up, making me look as if I'm giving inappropriate jesters to those walking by. Thankfully, Captain McSorley hasn't noticed. He's a man some say spawned from the lake itself, born with gills no less—quite comfortable at the helm. I'm glad he's here. I'd follow that man to the bottom of Lake Superior, and back again of course.

The gulls are acting odd. Most others on the crew don't see the significance. I, on the other hand, recognize the situation as peculiar to say the least. In most cases, the sea gulls, or Terns if you will, normally enjoy the nesting grounds of the nearby Saint Louis River near Duluth. But today they are busy swooping in a sporadic fashion directly at the *Mighty Fitz*, like it was some demonic entity bent on destroying their world. Of course, trudging through their waters with tons of iron ore might in fact be a form of destruction—if we sank that is. Or maybe the gulls were warning us of our dangerous predicament, that the gathering clouds above and the stinging winds would only get worse, to the point where the water gods would reveal themselves. Regardless, the gulls were pummeling us like Japanese Kamikaze pilots in WWII, not concerned about their own safety, only looking for the good of their fellow feathered friends.

Journal Entry: November 9, 1975, 7:04 p.m.

I fear for the worst now. The typical voyage which started only a few hours ago from dock number one in Superior, Wisconsin, had turned to anything but usual. The dark feeling inside me has spread to others in the crew. Not that we would discuss it—we didn't have to. You can see it in our glistening eyes, bulging with concern as we look between the thickening waves and wind. Sure, we're trying to ignore it; fear will only get in the way of our jobs, making it impossible to work. Perhaps this storm will be like all the others, ones the *Mighty Fitz* navigated swift and sure. Only time will tell, I suppose. Although I feel we may not have much of that left.

The environment on the *Fitz* has turned heavy, toxic even, yet still nobody stands up and voices their concern. Business as usual, with no interruptions. That's the only way to get through a storm like this. Current weather reports gale force winds. We didn't need a weather report to tell us that. We could see it with our own eyes. Still, we had a business to run, owned by Northwestern Mutual Life Insurance of Milwaukee, to transport iron ore and other precious commodities of the surrounding region. Having me spout off about the deranged behavior of a few seagulls, and the pain in my trick middle finger, well, that would only complicate things—not to mention delay payroll to feed my children. No, crying for help and pleading to turn about was not an option. That's not what a salty would do.

I must ignore my anxious feelings, no matter how terrifying. I must focus on the mind's logic, hoping it will guide me through these ugly thoughts. Sweat beads down my face, even with the temperature well below zero. I bite my tongue and continue my route as watchman, holding down that inner voice which wants to scream, "Get out! Abandon ship!"

Journal Entry: November 10, 1975, 3:10 p.m.

Snow has started to fall, adding to the misery and confusion swirling around us. Fifteen-foot waves are now crashing over the big *Fitz*, which I fear may not be

big enough for this storm. There is a howl in the wind unlike anything I've heard before. Almost like… the screams and shrieks of people? Perhaps they are the souls of all who perished in the depths of the Superior, howling their stories to all nearby—or maybe warning. Would we be next? I hoped for the best, praying for a calmer journey, though I wasn't a praying man. Yet now seemed as good a time as any to start.

Captain gave the order for bilge pumps to take the excess water out. While my job as watchman focused more on water, I couldn't help notice the dwindling morale of the crew—it seemed to be breaking apart with each crashing wave. I find myself peering into the snow as it blows horizontally across the swelling waves. The howling continues, now clearly sounding like something unnatural, and it seems now and then I catch a glimpse of something hovering above the waves, something not of this world—or any world that I'm familiar with. Perhaps it's just a sturgeon, or giant lake trout. No, this seemed more phantom like, large and ominous, as if perhaps Poseidon himself is visiting us.

There are stories of water gods visiting the Great Lakes. My grandfather used to talk about them, the ones that the Native Americans had in their legends. They were called Manitou, spirit gods, which will rise from the depths of the Great Lakes when angered, or when it was time to feed. I wondered if the Manitou now hungered for the *Fitz*. May God be with us.

Journal Entry: November 10, 1975, 7:15 p.m.

I huddle fearfully within the walls of my sleeping compartment, terrified of my most certain watery death and permanent entombment within the depths of the *Mighty Fitz*. Yet I must continue to write these words—not for my own safety as I am sadly sure the Manitou are out there and will take us soon. These words are for the survivors, not aboard this iron ship filled with an iron doom, but for the other saltys from other ships, tacking with a blind eye to what lurks beneath them. I now know that the water gods exist—*the Manitou are real*.

At first I thought my sight was mistaken, blurred by the water-spotted and ice-encrusted porthole I peered through. Maybe I was just carried away by the fear from the howls and shrieking beyond. But then those fiery eyes peered at me through the chilling ice storm. Something was out there, and I could sense it wanted me—trying to lure me out to my demise as huge waves crashed around us—the eyes of some demonic creature, born of water, ice, and evil energy incarnate. They locked on to me, seeming to read my thoughts and know for certain the fear shredding my heart. A thought stabbed into my chest like an icy sword as I watched the Manitou smile. Words smothered my mind that asked, *do you believe?*

At first I wondered what it meant, but then quickly surmised that the icy thing that swirled just beyond the comforts of my porthole both in mind and ship was asking about my belief in it. Did I believe in it—a supernatural and all-powerful being? Logic and reason screamed a triumphant no. Yet the dark reality unfolding around me, squelching other thoughts forming in my head, forced an answer in an echoed chorus of a thousand ghouls. The answer was a triumphant yes.

I know not why, but the water gods have not claimed us yet. Are they perhaps deciding what our fate should be? Are we sinners of evil cargo, traversing across their playground hauling a rotting carcass of ore, threatening to pollute their world? Perhaps. Or maybe they are just playing with us, watching our actions and thoughts like pawns on a chess board. Regardless, I have been given time to finish these words as they begin to search the *Mighty Fitz* for their newly found flesh and souls.

The waves now crash… far above… no hope… One can only…

History

Many have heard about the tragic voyage of the late *Edmund Fitzgerald*, heading out on its final journey from Duluth, Minnesota, sinking in a freak Lake Superior storm on November 10, 1975, and losing its entire crew of twenty-nine. But to this day, the actual demise of the *Edmund Fitzgerald* is still a mystery. The story above is but one of several possible theories.

The SS *Edmund Fitzgerald*, also known as the *Mighty Fitz*, was grand in many ways. Built in the late 1950s at 730 feet long, 75 feet wide, and 25 feet deep, it was originally the largest ship traversing the Great Lakes.

Named after the Northwestern President, Edmund Fitzgerald, the ship's life was plagued with misfortune from the beginning. On its christening and launch ceremony of June 7, 1958, the smashing of the champagne bottle over the bow took several attempts. Later, the shipyard crew struggled to release her from the keel blocks. Finally freed, it crashed violently into a nearby pier.

For many years the *Fitzgerald* carried taconite iron ore pellets from Duluth to Detroit or Toledo, setting hauling records numerous times. And with Captain Ernest M. McSorley at her command, she set sail on her final voyage from Superior, Wisconsin on November 9, 1975.

By the following day she was caught in a massive winter storm with hurricane-force winds and waves over thirty-five feet high. By 7:10 p.m., the *Fitzgerald* mysteriously sank in the Canadian waters 530 feet deep near Whitefish Bay. She had reported no difficulties and no distress signals prior to sinking. All twenty-nine crew members perished, and there were no bodies recovered.

Numerous theories have been explored over the years, all examining the reason why such a mighty ship could sink so quickly. The most plausible theory is that a huge rogue wave struck her, causing catastrophic failure and swamping the ship beyond resolution. Other possibilities involve water seeping in through cargo hatches and the deck, or topside destruction from the waves, or even being shoaled in the shallow part of Lake Superior. Regardless of its demise, it's one of the most noted disasters of the Great Lakes, especially since the Gordon Lightfoot 1976 hit song, "The Wreck of the *Edmund Fitzgerald*."

What we do know about the *Fitzgerald's* final voyage is that it left Superior, Wisconsin at 2:15 p.m. on November 9, 1975, commanded by Captain Ernest M. McSorley, on route to Zug Island near Detroit. Around 5 p.m., she joined another ship, the *Arthur M. Anderson*, on its way from Two Harbors, Minnesota to Gary, Indiana. The weather forecast indicated a storm would be arriving in the morning the next day.

A nearby ship, the SS *Wilfred Sykes*, recorded the initial conversations over the radio between the *Fitzgerald* and the *Anderson*. By 7 p.m., the weather service had issued a gale force wind warning for all of Lake Superior. The ships then went north for shelter in the Canadian coast. By 1 a.m., they were in the middle of a massive winter storm, with winds at 60 MPH and waves topping over ten feet.

By the morning, the faster *Fitzgerald* had pulled ahead of the *Anderson*, with the intensity of the massive winter storm increasing. The *Anderson* lost sight of the *Fitzgerald* by the afternoon. By mid-afternoon, Captain McSorley of the *Fitzgerald* radioed the *Anderson* to report taking on water and that the vessel had developed a list. Shortly afterward, the *Fitz* had lost its radar, and its bilge pumps began failing.

The *Anderson* directed the *Fitzgerald* to Whitefish Bay for safety, however the *Mighty Fitz* was perhaps already too far gone. Captain McSorley was heard over the radio stating, "I have a bad list; I have lost both radars and am taking heavy seas over the deck in one of the worst seas I have ever been in."

By late afternoon, nearby ships had recorded gusts of wind over eighty-five MPH, and rogue waves over thirty-five feet high. The final radio signal from the *Mighty Fitz* came at just after 7 p.m. on November 10, 1975. Captain McSorley reported that, "We are holding our own." Minutes later she mysteriously sank, disappearing from both radio and radar for good.

As stated, the most plausible cause of the big *Fitz'* sinking was due to the massive winter storm's winds and waves. But some speculate further into what caused the devastating storm. Typical weather patterns may be the culprit, with random chance involved. Or perhaps, as the story in the beginning of this chapter alludes to, it may have been something more—the work of the Lake Superior Water Gods.

The Native Americans around Lake Superior knew about the many water gods, or Manitous, thriving in the area. The Native Americans would pay their homage to them, sending ornaments, tobacco, and other artifacts into the water, where one of the Manitous lived. Whether it was Manibozho, on the north shore near Thunder Cape, or La Chapelle, among the Pictured Rocks, powerful rulers of the mighty storms existed, sending fear to any daring to voyage across the great unsalted sea.

The Chippewa, at Keweenaw Point, believed demons would visit unless proper artifacts and treasures would be given, dropped into the depths of the lake where the evil lived. And yet another devilish Manitou lived near the mouth of Superior Bay. It is said this spirit lives at the bottom of the lake, always gazing upward for unsuspecting prey who dare to voyage across her domain.

So as one can surmise, while most believe the *Mighty Edmund Fitzgerald* sank to the depths of Lake Superior due to hurricane force winds and rogue waves, few question *where* the storm came from. Perhaps the demons of the Great Lakes? An impish Manitou, hungry for the fresh souls of a passing ship? Of course, there's only one way to find out. Why not take a trip across the great unsalted sea? Let me know what you come up with. Then again, if you never return, I'll know the answer.

The Glensheen Mansion of Duluth, Minnesota, where ghosts from the past go bump in the night.

CHAPTER 3

Glensheen Ghosts
of Duluth

I used to work at the Glensheen Mansion, employed as a tour guide—but not anymore. Not since I saw Elisabeth's haunting eyes in the dead of night.

Don't get me wrong—there's no doubt that Elisabeth Congdon was a sweet and joyful lady. In talking with psychics, they say it's no different in the afterlife. However, it's a terrifying experience to be locking up late at night by yourself and have a full-body apparition floating in front of you.

I never believed in ghosts. When I first heard that the Glensheen Mansion was haunted, I scoffed at the idea. I was more freaked out by the murders that took place in the mansion. Shivers went down my spine every time I walked into the billiard room, thinking about the intruder breaking in and committing murder shortly thereafter.

My first ghostly experience seemed more of an afterthought. As a tour guide, you sometimes have to lock up late at night after the last tour, along with going room to room checking on the place. Once the sun sets, we have lights on in every room of the mansion. When the last tour comes through, we turn the lights off. However, one time I noticed on my way out that a light was still on in an upstairs bedroom.

I returned to the mansion to shut the light off, when a strange feeling came over me—one filled with sadness and depression. I didn't think much of it at the time; I was more interested in turning off the light and getting out.

The next event was a bit more serious. This dealt with your classic "shadow figures." As I have said, I never believed in ghosts and the things that go bump in the night. But the night I saw the shadow figure floating through the upstairs hallway, well, that changed everything.

I talked with other tour guides, hoping they could help make sense of what I saw, to explain with a rational and logical mind that the shadows I saw were nothing more than a figment of my imagination. Unfortunately, they had seen them, too.

On the one hand, it was a relief that others had this same experience. Then again, it meant that just maybe ghosts and ghouls were real. Still, I wasn't ready to shift my belief and shrugged the paranormal incident off. After all, I couldn't just quit, scared of some silly ghost stories. I needed the money to help finish off my English degree at the University of Minnesota Duluth. Little did I know I should have listened to my inner sense and run like hell.

Flickering lights and shadow figures continued to haunt my world at the Glensheen Mansion. I tried my best to ignore them, but the more I avoided what was happening, the worst it got. Soon the experiences were happening in broad daylight and with a full tour group.

"Did you see that?" asked a little boy while he held his mom's hand. He made a fluttering jester, flapping his hands up and down while moving his arms to the left. His expression seemed intense, devilish almost, not like something you would see on your typical boy of about ten years old. The little boy turned to me and asked, "You saw it, didn't you?"

Of course I saw it. The shadow darted from the corner of my eye down the dimly lit hallway, pausing only for a moment, as if mocking me. I smiled and ignored the boy's comment, continuing with the tour. After all, we were not allowed to discuss anything about the murder—and certainly not the ghostly visits occurring on a frequent basis.

I actually agreed with the policy. It's quite amazing, all the positive things the Congdon family had provided to the community of Duluth, not to mention the entire state of Minnesota and Midwest. No, the important thing for the tours was to let others know about the philanthropic life they offered, as well as the luxurious world of the rich and famous back in the early 1900s. Of course, none of that changed the shift in reality happening to me. I soon believed in ghosts wholeheartedly, and I was about to get the ultimate paranormal experience of my life.

As the incidents continued, and I accepted this new supernatural realm, I decided to research why this was happening. Not from a paranormal perspective, like they do on the Sy-Fy channel's *Ghost Hunter*, or Travel Channel's *Ghost Adventure*. This was more on a personal level, as in why are the ghosts haunting me at Glensheen Mansion?

I started with the history, how the Congdon family moved from New York to Chippewa Falls, Wisconsin, and eventually Duluth, with a law practice in place and becoming avid capitalists. However, it seemed to me the real trouble began later with the adoption of Marjorie. As anyone familiar with the Glensheen Mansion knows, based on the many books and blogs on the Glensheen murder incident, Marjorie was at the forefront of speculation.

Further research began to show a pattern of sociological concerns for the adopted Marjorie. But I went beyond that. Just because you are adopted doesn't mean you get involved with murder and possibly arson. Could there be something more to this? I wasn't sure, but the thought definitely concerned me, wondering if perhaps worse things had happened to Marjorie, causing her to spiral down a wicked path of no return. I even thought she might be dealing with demonic possession, although I could never find any proof. It makes you wonder if that's how the rich and famous in life get to where they are—by making deals with the devil.

The hauntings continued. If anything, they got worse, polarizing on my newly found belief in the unbelievable, with me perhaps acting like a catalyst. There seemed to be weekly occurrences of shadowy figures in the upstairs hallway or that dreaded feeling of being watched when you know you're alone in the mansion. It didn't matter whether I was cleaning up after a long day of tours or just simply resting quietly in a vacant room—the feeling was there. Eventually, that eerie sense of someone behind you—inches from you—got the best of me, making me gasp or scream. Of course, every time I turned to look, nothing would be there.

I finally had the last straw, happening the week before Christmas. We were preparing for several tours during the festive season, pulling out all the stops and setting up Christmas decorations throughout the mansion, complete with a seriously oversized Christmas tree. Of course, the boxes of holiday goodies were stored in the creepy basement—the last place I wanted to go.

I avoided the damp, dark basement like the black plague. Up to that point I had not experienced anything alarming down there—yet others had. It was the usual shadow figures from the corner of your eye, or an oppressing feeling of dread, or as if some mischievous creature was crouched in a dark corner waiting for you to shuffle by—possibly for the last time.

The lighting in the basement seemed to be lit with medieval torchlights at best, but that was no concern of mine. I always brought a flashlight with me, checking repeatedly as I entered the darkness to ensure the light stick worked. What alarmed me most was the recent information I'd discovered while doing my paranormal research. Ghosts liked to drain batteries. That meant my flashlight could be instantly drained of energy, making it as useless as plastic stakes at a vampire convention. That's why I carried extra batteries in my pocket. I just hoped the ghosts didn't notice them.

The Christmas decorations needed were ropes of garland in boxes, used to spruce up the main staircase. There seemed to be an endless parade of boxes, due to the length of steps involved. Not that I had the opportunity to retrieve all of them. After the first box...I was done.

The basement on any given day would be cold and clammy. This morning, however, it was exceptionally chilly. Not just because it was December in Duluth, with a frosty wind blowing across Lake Superior and pummeling the mansion. No, this was different. This chill seemed to come from within the basement—from within me maybe, as I stepped off the staircase onto the basement floor.

As luck would have it, the boxes were on the opposite side, making me slowly shuffle through the entire length of the basement, flashlight in hand and ready for use, even with the lights functioning flawlessly. That is until I reached the first box.

Everything went dreamlike—in a nightmarish sort of way. It didn't seem like this could be happening to me. Yet there I was; the basement lights flickered twice and went out. I swung around the room with my flashlight, darting back and forth off the nearby walls, waiting for some demon to show its ugly face. While no demons appeared, something else did that terrified me just the same.

It's one thing to hear voices that aren't there, or see shadow figures zipping around at the edge of your vision. Or even when things seem to be misplaced or moved. All these things could be considered paranormal, but when weeks and months pass by, you question yourself, trying hard to find other explanations—ones involving logic and reason. What I experienced down in the basement of the Glensheen Mansion that morning defies all things logical and reasonable. That's what happens when you come face to face with a ghost.

In my mind I feel like the ghostly apparition hovering only a few feet from me looked hideous, with faded and drooping flesh and ashen eyes sunk so deep into the skull, they were barely noticeable. Or that the body was seriously putrid, with flesh and muscle barely hanging from bone, like something from a classic zombie movie.

No, in reality it was simply a normal looking person. Sure, it was faded, translucent, and hovering above the ground, but the features of the body were quite normal. Regardless, it terrified me all the same. It really boils down to being there, in the dark, knowing nothing was there a second ago, and then *bam*! Full-body apparition. It was only for a second or two, but it felt like an eternity. The figure was definitely that of an old lady. I'm sure it was Elisabeth Congdon—maybe trying to help me with the boxes. Or perhaps the nurse that was murdered, still ready and willing to lend a helping hand. Either way, I was out of there, never to return.

History

The Glensheen Mansion, built in 1908, is one of the most mysterious places and most talked about locations in Northern Minnesota. Especially among those searching for ghosts. Why? Mostly because of the tragedy, with befalling Elisabeth Congdon and her nurse who were brutally murdered, left to die in the mansion.

Construction of the mansion began in 1905 by Chester Congdon, naming it Glensheen, which means "shining glen," after his ancestral home in Surrey, England. The mansion was finished by 1908, costing nearly one million dollars, a sizable amount for most people during the turn of the century—but not for Mr. Congdon and his lawyer profession. Overlooking the shores of Lake Superior, it was the envy of Duluth and the surrounding areas. That is until the tragic occurrences of the late 1970s...

Elisabeth Congdon, age 83 and daughter of the late Chester Congdon, was found dead on June 27, 1977, suffocated in bed with a pillow. Her nurse, Velma Pietila was also murdered, bludgeoned to death on a stair landing with a candlestick. It appears as though the murderer came through a window in the billiard room, threw the nurse down the stairs, and then suffocated Elisabeth with a pillow.

As it turns out, Elisabeth had an adopted daughter, Marjorie, who was next in line to inherit Elisabeth's large fortune. And soon after the murder, Marjorie's husband was accused and finally convicted of the murders. However, the conviction was overturned a few years later. Marjorie was also tried and acquitted.

Yet after Marjorie's husband was released from prison, he was found dead under mysterious circumstances. Marjorie was charged initially, but later the charges were dropped—although she is currently in prison for attempted arson. Ultimately, the case of the Glensheen murders is unsolved.

So, what really happened? Or does it matter? Obviously a murder occurred. And for anyone interested in the paranormal, the Glensheen Mansion is no doubt ripe for investigation. Yet, to date, the establishment, currently owned by the University of Minnesota, states that the mansion is not haunted. Others, though, beg to differ.

The Glensheen Mansion is reported to be haunted by Elisabeth Congdon, as well as her nurse Velma. Numerous former workers (mostly tour guides) have commented on the haunting incidents. Most notably, the ghostly mist of Elisabeth can be seen in the Library, reading books she enjoyed so many times while living.

Frequent paranormal events reported are:

- Screams can be heard after hours, as if the murders are still taking place.
- Shadowy figures can be seen gliding across the halls and basement, as well as a feeling of being watched.
- Other incidents report moaning sounds or ghostly orbs floating through the air. Most of this occurs to the workers on site after hours.
- The guest room at the west end on the third floor is extremely active, with lots of poltergeist-like incidents.
- Reports of lights flickering on and off by themselves in many rooms across the mansion, especially in the library and basement.
- Some have claimed to see two women standing in the upstairs windows, looking out through the trees toward Lake Superior (reportedly caught in a photograph). There is also a report of candy being moved back and forth over a dresser.
- One phenomenon is of a strange and eerie feeling, filled with sadness and terror when visiting the area where Elisabeth and Velma died.

- The main staircase and its landing have been known to occupy a phantom lady dressed in period clothing, similar to clothes taken during a photo shoot for a Christmas promo.
- Also, the large luggage closet and the south end of the attic are very active.

So, it seems something is going on at the Glensheen Mansion, and I highly suggest you tour the location. Just don't ask about the ghosts—they won't talk about them. Your best bet is to bring an audio recorder with you and try to find some paranormal experiences of your own. As you tour, keep your recorder turned on so that you can listen to it later. You may find that you were not alone and that you've captured some haunting electronic voice phenomena (EVP). There's nothing better than firsthand experiences—assuming you live to tell about them.

CHAPTER 4

Monster Moose of Thunder Bay

One of the many signs warning you of moose around Thunder Bay, Ontario, Canada. Some small, some big—some monster-size big.

Monsters come in all different shapes and sizes. Some are composed of putrid ugliness; others will lure you away with their impeccable beauty. Regardless, the outcome when confronted by their fiendishness is the same; you are left with feelings of horror and terror. My weekend with a monster moose ended up no different.

The plan was for me and my girlfriend to have one of those great northern Minnesota getaway weekends. Being she was from Superior, Wisconsin, and I was then from Duluth, Minnesota, our version of "somewhere north" meant Canada—Thunder Bay, Ontario to be exact.

"Let's do something different Ray," stated Sammy as we waited in line at the Burger King off West Superior Street in downtown Duluth. Spring break was coming up for the University of Minnesota Duluth (go Bulldogs!).

While most sane college students have thoughts of spending the break somewhere down south, such as Fort Lauderdale or the Padre Islands, our budget kept us somewhere closer to home. Both of us loved to downhill ski, or I should say one of us. Sammy was an avid snowboarder, ready in a moment's notice to shred some snow. As for me, strapping two boards onto my feet seemed to give me better odds in the stability department.

The previous year we stayed on campus. Sure we had fun, but it wasn't anything amazing, other than not having to do homework. Sammy and I had known each other for almost sixteen months, after hooking up at a house party off East Toledo Street. They had an indoor beach party where a ton of sand was brought in and spread across the entire first floor of the house. Definitely a fun time, especially since the outside temperature hovered just below freezing. But what did you expect for a chilling November day in Minnesota?

"We should go skiing," blurted Sammy as we studied for our English final in the library, just across from the Labovitz School of Business building. Sammy's major was business, mine computers. Still, we both had to pass the general education English class. Otherwise our spring break would be dismal at best.

We skied at Spirit Mountain numerous times in the past, and even made a couple trips to Lutsen Ski Resort. However, Sammy wanted something different.

"How about Canada," I asked. It seemed reasonable, and definitely close enough to keep the cost down.

"What, like up with the polar bears?"

She wasn't the sharpest tool in the shed, but I liked her nonetheless. "No, not that far north. Nothing like the north pole." I thought for a moment. "Must be something just north of the boarder. Thunder Bay maybe?"

"That sounds like fun!" yelled Sammy as she leaned over and kissed me amidst the shushing of others in the library.

So it was set. Skiing in Canada, Thunder Bay Ontario. To me the best resort looked like Mount Baldy—not to be confused with the Mount Baldy of Philmont, New Mexico. Still, it had a decent elevation and, while there were only a few lifts and runs, several were long enough to have some fun on them.

Spring break finally arrived and we were off on our mini-expedition to the north, an international trip for two. It would take just under four hours of driving, that is if we didn't stop. Of course there would be several excursions along the way. After all, this was spring break—we were here to enjoy. Some of the notable planned stops were Betty's Pies, the Black Woods Restaurant in Two Harbors, Gooseberry Falls, Split Rock Light House, just to name a few. No, even though we left bright and early Saturday morning, it would take all day to arrive in Thunder Bay.

While the trip encountered fun throughout the day, it by no means was strenuous or thrilling. Although, I have to admit, Betty's Pies were thrilling to the taste buds. Actually, most of the suspense involved discussions around who would win the Super Bowl next year—the Packers or the Vikings. After much debate, we concluded, as of late, that the Packers would surely win. However, I could not let the up-and-coming powers of the Vikings go unnoticed; they would be in the Super Bowl once again—hopefully before the turn of the next century. Of course, Sammy, being a loyal Packer fan, pushed the "who won the most Super Bowls" issue. Yes, in the end, the Packers have won more. I quickly changed the subject, not wanting to dwell on the zero and four record the Vikings have in Super Bowls.

"Can you imagine coming through this region back before cars and airplanes?" I asked.

"Or cell phones," added Sammy. "Not to mention the ability to text."

"Yeah, but our reception won't be the best where we are going, way out in Thunder Bay."

"What would Paul Bunyan do?" asked Sammy.

I looked at her, confused, giving her that "I don't have a clue what you're talking about" look. "What?" I said.

She repeated, "Paul Bunyan. You know, that lumberjack guy before all this technology happened. I wonder what it was like for him."

I nodded, unable to articulate any reasonable response. I suppose he'd use a laptop as a cell phone.

"I bet there were gigantic moose back then," she said. "Bigger than a house."

Both of us looked out the windshield high above, picturing a moose that tall. Little did we know how close to the truth we were.

We made it through the Canadian border past Grand Portage on Highway 61 without a hitch. Although we had to toss the case of Budweiser going through customs, apparently that was a threatening species in Canada. Neither of us had been to another country before, so the experience rolling through the border patrol was intense. Then again, it's not a problem getting out of the U.S.; it's always trying to get back in.

With all the sightseeing along the way, it had turned dark by the time we crossed the border and continued on Highway 61. I started thinking about hitting a deer or bear, and then remembered the moose, that "other" animal to watch out for in the upper regions of North America. They were far worse to hit, especially since the bulk of their body is at windshield level, propped up on slender, toothpick-like legs.

"Moose Hill!" exclaimed Sammy as she pointed at the sign. "We should go look for one!"

I slammed on the brakes instinctively, then tried not to roll my eyes at her. Just because the name was Moose Hill didn't necessarily mean there were moose running around. Then again, it didn't indicate there wouldn't be. Sammy rested her hand on my leg and said, "Take that road. I bet there are *Meeses* there!"

It was only 8 p.m. According to my calculations, we weren't that far from Thunder Bay and the ski resort. Spending a few minutes on a side trip down a deserted road can't hurt too much, right? Little did I know…

Within a couple of minutes down Tower Road, Sammy was stretched over to me, nibbling at my ear. Apparently, she wasn't that interested in moose anymore. Just as I was about to pull over and nibble back, we struck it. "It" being one gigantic-sized moose. Actually, I didn't know *what* it was at first—just something tall, thick, and hairy. I must point out here that we actually didn't "hit it." We went *under* it. That's how big it was.

Of course, it helped to be driving a little puddle-jumper car, a Fiat 500, that could probably fit under a cow, or maybe even a pig. Regardless, we both screamed as we slid underneath the beast. The car spun around several times on the frosted road before landing with a crumpled crunch in the ditch.

We had been wearing seat belts, which probably saved our lives, along with the airbags. Or so I thought. I turned to look back at the towering beast on the road, only to find it charging at us, snorting with wisps of steam the whole way. If it weren't for the seat belts and airbags, we could have easily hopped out and run for cover. Instead, we spent what felt like an eternity trying to free ourselves from the seat belts.

Just when I thought the monstrous moose would be eating us for a light, evening snack, it disappeared. We looked around, wondering where the thing had gone. We eventually got free from our seat belts, hopped out of the car, and surveyed the situation. It was obvious some kind of super large animal had been there. There were hoof marks to prove it. I could see where it charged at us, and then simply disappeared. "Either that moose can fly, or we just had a mass hallucination," I said.

"But there's only two of us," replied Sammy.

"Two is still plural; remember our English class?" As far as I was concerned, "mass" meant more than one. Regardless, we had to get the car out of the ditch and be on our way. After repeated attempts to free it from the confines of the deep snowy ditch, we reluctantly gave up.

"Now what?" asked Sammy.

I pulled out my cell phone, readying myself to call Triple A. Unfortunately, there was no signal. Either we had stopped in a dead zone for wireless signals, or I had forgotten to pay my phone bill. Either explanation was certainly plausible. I looked around in the darkness, with only the moon and stars poking through the clouds giving us light. Far in the distance, I could see a light. I pointed toward the direction, with her acknowledging it. "Let's head that way. Maybe there's a phone."

As we trudged through the snow toward the glowing orb in the distance, I couldn't help but think about the moose we had run over, or in our case run under. As we walked, I could hear something behind us casting deep snorts and rumbling breaths. It didn't sound good. I walked faster, not wanting to stop and address the menacing sounds. No, moving toward the light—into the light—was my prime directive.

Within a few minutes, we had reached the light. As it turned out, the orb of safety was a light hanging above the porch of a rustic cabin, built from nearby pine, no doubt. I politely knocked on the door, sending echoing thumps through the silent and frosty landscape. Almost silent that is. I could still here snorts from somewhere in the darkness behind us. Sammy could hear them, too, showing me her bulging eyes, but not daring to turn around and look for the source.

I refused to be intimidated by my childish fears, which was probably the first mistake of my many mistakes that night. I turned to look and, in the pale blue moon light, I could see something large lurking among the tall pines, snorting and grunting like a dark demon hunting its prey. I knew it was the moose, but wondered why it stalked us. *Why would a moose do that?* No normal moose would, then again I doubted it was anything typical.

I turned away, focusing on the door that stood between the safety of the cabin and the behemoth lumbering moose. "Nobody's home," I said as I reached for the door handle.

"We can't go in," said Sammy while slapping my hand away from the door. More snorting erupted from behind. She briefly turned to look, but then quickly yanked the door handle instead. Thankfully, the door opened, allowing us safe harbor. Of course, who's to say the monstrous moose wouldn't demolish the tiny frozen hut. Then again, we didn't have too many options. At the moment, I had no desire, nor means to battle the creature or slay it.

We settled into the cabin, hoping the pine log walls were enough to prevent the moose from getting in. Listening fearfully, we questioned our sanity as we heard nothing outside. We pondered that perhaps our senses had failed us, simply hallucinating the oversized moose. Yet soon the snorting sounds erupted, grunting with defiance. It lurked beyond the door for sure, even if we could not see it.

I looked across the central room of the cabin, dimly lit by the flickering red emergency light above the front door. I lost myself for a moment, wondering if the emergency light was powered by batteries or perhaps solar. Grunts from beyond snapped my apathy, letting me focus on the tasks to keep us safe. The walls would protect us—at least that's what I thought.

I quickly began checking for weapons. While I hoped to find some seriously large filet knives, I at least found comfort in the pre-civil war, musket-loading rifle above the mantle. Only time would tell. Although, I wondered how much time we had. *Would the moose eventually go away?* We hoped so. Unfortunately, the crazed moose had other ideas: waiting for us all night.

Hours had passed and our stomachs began to rumble. We managed to find a few cans of beans in the cupboard, as well as sauerkraut. Nothing against anyone German, but I could think of a thousand better ways to prepare cabbage, other than pickling it in brine. Regardless, we were happy to be nourished. Water, on the other hand, became the bigger issue.

They say you can survive weeks without food, but only a few days without water. Unfortunately for us, within the confines of the cabin any realistic form of water could not be found. "I'm thirsty," whispered Sammy, trying to keep from stirring the giant moose outside. This had not been her first water request. That had occurred hours ago. Now, in the morning before sunrise, she had become a bit more serious.

I knew my only option would be to venture forth into the darkness and collect some snow. It should be easy, right? How fast could a moose run? I'm sure I could dart out into the frozen shadowy landscape to scoop a pile of snow. I would be fine, provided I didn't think about the moose lurking in the icy gloom, waiting for me to play. I had no desire to do anything with the great northern ox, yet it most certainly had other ideas.

It seemed to be playing with me—letting me leave the cabin and fill my frying pan with snow. With my confidence rising, I strutted slowly back to the cabin, like a rooster who's just finished mating. That's when the moose revealed itself. At first, I just heard snorting, but then the gnashing of its large teeth became apparent. Seconds later, I could hear loud, swooshing sounds as its gigantic antlers swung back and forth above me, slashing and stabbing. I can't say for sure the size of the creature, as I never took the time to look back. Based on the thunderous stomping it made, and the grunting from above, it had to be over ten feet tall.

Thankfully, I made it to the porch, leaping to safety. The large rack of antlers swooped down at me, becoming wedged between the posts of the porch, giving me just enough time to dive through the cabin door. The moose, obviously perturbed, shrieked and twisted as it tried to free itself. I thought it might demolish the cabin in the process. Luckily, only the porch crumbled, leaving our benevolent abode intact.

In no time, Sammy had the stove working, fed from the propane tank outside the cabin. With the snow melted, we drank heartily, as if feasting at a royal banquet. We tried eating more beans but refrained from any additional sauerkraut. The beans were bad enough, surely making for a gaseous morning; adding fermented cabbage would only make things worse.

Eventually, the call of the wild reared its ugly head, and both of us had to use the bathroom. Of course the only facilities were outside, beyond the luxuries of our pine-partitioned security—outside where the moose lurked.

Being the chivalrous guy that I am, I volunteered to stand watch outside as Sammy used the outhouse. We found a small flashlight in a kitchen drawer to help with our late night adventure, but it barely lit the ground in front of us as we moved quietly across the snowy ground. Most importantly, I found no signs of the moose. *Perhaps it got bored with us?* Sammy finished her business in the rustic port-a-potty, signaled by the slamming of the lid. She smiled coming out and said, "Oh wait, I forgot to flush."

"Funny," I replied as I entered the commode, glad to see our spirits were more upbeat. Yet no sooner had I dropped my pants when all hell broke loose—in a *ginormous* moosing sort of way.

It might have helped if Sammy had guarded the outhouse, warning me of the impending doom. Then again, it might have only made things worse. Sammy, in her infinite wisdom, decided to go in the cabin, leaving me alone—sort of. I could hear snorts and grunts from beyond the outhouse door.

"Sammy?" I asked into the darkness as the flashlight went totally dead. No response. Without any warning, the sides of the outhouse exploded, not by the doings of anything methane, but by the power of the demonic moose. The outhouse, with me in it, flew through the air and landed hard, splintering into a pile of stinky lumber. The two rolls of toilet paper landed near me, having soared through the air like New Year's Eve streamers.

I scrambled out of the shredded lumber quietly, hoping the moose would not notice me. Thankfully, the moose turned its attention to the hole in the ground where the outhouse once stood, sniffing and sneezing as it poked around.

I knew I had to act quickly and sprinted back to the safety of the cabin. With my pants not quite up, I bolted for the door. The remaining lumber pieces flew in every direction. This apparently confused the moose and gave me the element of surprise. Unfortunately, it didn't take long for the hulking moose to catch up, with its snout still sneezing from the contents of the outhouse hole.

I could have easily made it inside, if it weren't for my pants. As I neared what remained of the porch, my pants dropped to my ankles and I stumbled up the steps. Yet that blunder might have saved my life. With me floundering on the porch floor, the moose tried to slow down, sending him off balance into the side of the cabin. That gave me the chance to lunge through the cabin door. I leaped forward, pants flapping around my ankles, as I finally got a good glimpse of the moose.

While it looked proportionate to any other moose, composed of a large snout and antlers, and big billiard ball eyes, the overall size went beyond description; it could easily tower over a large pickup truck. What sent shivers down my spine were the color of its eyes: crimson red and flaring, like some demonic creature.

Sammy slammed the door shut, stared at me for a moment, and then sniffed. "You stink."

I'm sure I did, what with rolling around in the splintered lumber of the outhouse. I ignored her comment, turning my attention to the monstrous moose outside. Yet once again, the creature seemed to disappear. We listened then looked through the windows—it was as silent and pristine as any frosty winter night.

We huddled together near the fireplace trying to keep warm for the remainder of the night. The sun began to rise just about the time we drifted off to sleep. That's when we heard a knock at the door.

"Anybody in there?" said a voice from outside before continuing to knock.

I stood up and peered through the window and could clearly see a uniformed officer. At first I was relieved to have something out there that didn't sport a giant pair of antlers. But then I worried for the safety of the policeman. Opening the door quickly, I said, "You better get in. Not safe out there."

The officer looked at me with raised eyebrows. Then he looked around at the demolished porch and cautiously stepped inside.

We explained our predicament to him, all the while staring out into the yard for any signs of our furry friend Bullwinkle. The officer kept calm, helping us to calm down as well, and eventually convinced us that we were safe and that we had a comfortable squad car waiting for us by our wrecked car. We were less than a mile away from town and could get a tow truck as well as a rental car. Just as we agreed to go with him to the car, taking just a few steps out into the frozen front yard, the moose attacked.

It came from nowhere, like a frosty spirit of an arctic wind, its eyes filled with red fury and its nostrils sending spirals of piping hot steam into the air. Sammy and I were expecting the monster moose to appear, but the policeman did not. He stood there in disbelief while we ran back into the safety of the cabin.

I looked briefly behind to see the moose jab with his antlers at the policeman, scooping him up like the shovel on a front loader. I closed my eyes in terror, but could not block out the screams of the officer as the moose carried him far into the forest beyond the cabin.

The entire day went by with no further sign of our demonic moose. We dared not venture beyond the cabin, not even for bathroom breaks. Not that there was anything left of the outhouse. We spent most of the day struggling to eat from the remaining cans of sauerkraut and trying to keep warm near the fireplace, speculating as to when the firewood would run out.

I had more concern for the lack of water. With no water, we knew we would eventually have to leave. If only we had a weapon of some kind, and maybe a torch or two. The torches were easy to concoct. We used a couple legs from the dining table, and cloth from the quilt on the bed. We found some kerosene in the cupboard near the front door.

As for weapons, two came to mind. The obvious one hung prominently on display above the fireplace mantle. The muzzle loading rifle probably had not been used for eons, not to mention the lack of gunpowder. I doubt the gun would scare off the monster moose, but we figured it couldn't hurt trying. The other weapon we found in the silverware drawer of the kitchen, a large knife used to filet fish.

The knife would do just fine, although it meant using it in close contact, which I doubted would work well. The knife and my arm had to be at least three feet shorter than the killer moose' antlers, not to mention I only had one sharp pointy object; the moose had at least a dozen.

We ended up fastening the knife to another leg from the table, which would keep me an additional two feet away from the moose. Not that it probably mattered. Two feet, ten feet, it all added up to a bad plan from an even worse idea, making me wonder if things couldn't get any more dismal. They did.

As the sun began to settle beneath the tree line, we decided to venture forth from the safety of the cottage, torches lit and ready, hoping the moose had moved on to other prey. After all, there had to be other unsuspecting tourists who had smashed up their car and were held captive in a strange cabin, right? We confidently marched across the snowy yard, me with a torch in one hand, and a make-shift spear in the other, praying the moose had vacated. It hadn't.

Within seconds, we knew trouble had found us in the form of a gigantic furry-but-not-so-cute creature, namely the beastly moose, charging at us like it had been waiting just beyond site. Or maybe this moose could be something even more horrific—a phantom creature of the night? Able to materialize at will anywhere it wanted? Regardless, we quickly stumbled back into the cabin, but not before Sammy dropped her torch on the porch. It quickly ignited the antique dry pine, sending flames across the floorboards and up the side of the cabin. We watched from inside as the heat intensified and the fire roared across the roof. I looked around, desperate for an escape route. I pointed to the back window and said, "Time to go."

Sammy gave me that *are you nuts?* look, but reluctantly agreed it would be better outside fighting a giant moose than to be inside roasting alive. Maybe.

We broke through the window and dived into the darkness, just as the cabin roof came crashing down. With a flickering torch in one hand and my filet knife spear in the other, we began our quest through the snow in search of the nearby town, praying that we would avoid any further confrontations with the monster moose.

We could see glowing lights in the distance, off the overcast sky. It was our best option, or maybe or only option at this point. It had to be the nearby town, or at least another safe harbor spot to regroup. We turned back briefly to see the glowing fire of the cabin we had just left. Unfortunately, we also heard snorting and grunting from there, too.

The moose stormed upon us, its phantom physique darting out of the darkness from all sides. One moment it snorted from behind, the next it grunted from in front. We never saw it, making me wonder, once again, if this was just some spirit monster terrorizing us more from within the confines of our mind. *Were we hallucinating all of this?* It didn't take long for me to get an answer.

After what seemed like hours of trudging through the snow toward the distant glowing lights, which appeared to be no closer, the torch ran out of fuel. We were left in the darkness, with only the dim light of the moon poking out from a group of silvery clouds.

The moose snorted violently, as if signaling his triumph. Then it shrieked—I will never forget the sound—something I'd never heard before, nor since. The shriek started as a low gravely rumble, then rose in pitch like a wailing siren. Then, the berserker moose charged at us, its thick harness of bony antlers bearing down hard. With death close at hand, I instinctively jumped to the side at the last minute, yet Sammy was not so lucky. She caught the full force of the antlers, getting tossed high into the air and landing among the distant tall pines, screaming the entire way.

I turned back to the beastly moose, who, in no time, had swiftly moved to where Sammy lay, towering over her and snorting like a wicked demon. The moose cocked its head, then sniffed at Sammy's limp body. With a victorious snort, the moose moved away from Sammy to focused on me—its next victim.

As the crazed moose charged, I quickly ran through my options. The only obvious choice that came to mind seemed idiotic at best. I thought about how, with a bear, you might try to play dead. Of course, that might either confuse the moose, or maybe annoy it. Either way, I was probably going to be dead, so I figured playing dead couldn't make the situation worse.

As the moose came upon me I dropped to the ground, unmoving. I kept my eyes tightly shut; the last thing I wanted to do was see the demon face, with its hot steaming nostrils and crimson-red, softball-sized eyes. I could feel it breathing on me, looming over me, shifting side to side, as if slowly inspecting its freshly caught prey. Just as I thought it would either eat me or give up and walk away, it shrieked again, this time chomping its teeth that sent crunching noises echoing into the surrounding forest. I waited for death, sure that I would be its next meal. At the last moment, I opened my eyes to see the monstrous moose raising its head and massive antlers, and knew I had but one chance. With both hands, I grabbed my filet knife spear and thrust it into its neck.

The moose reared back in pain, bolting away before quickly dropping a few yards from me. *Did I just kill a monster moose?* I forced myself up and shuffled my way over to the lifeless moose. Sure enough, the beast was dead.

The tables had turned—now I was the one shrieking with victory. I screamed in triumph, then fell silent as I heard my echoes reverberate through the pine-laden forest. Then, from nearby, I could hear the faint sounds of moaning.

Sammy had woken up, and quickly began complaining about my screaming, not to mention her serous headache and the frigid temperatures. I realized we would need to find a shelter immediately, or even with conquering a demonic moose, we would soon be dead ourselves from the frigid temperatures. It had to be well below zero and, without the warmth of a torch or fire, we would expire within minutes. That's when I pointed to the moose and said, "In there."

"What?" asked Sammy, standing there in disbelief as I began carving up the monster moose, gutting it to make room for us inside. The filet knife spear proved to be very sharp and made quick work. "Don't worry," I said, "I've seen this in the movies."

"Okay, Rambo," she replied, "but I'm not getting in there." She turned and began walking into the forest.

Angry, tired, and frustrated, I said, "Suit yourself. But don't come crawling back to me expecting to snuggle in the moose." I doubted I would ever see her again.

Within minutes I had made a shelter out of the moose carcass and slid comfortably inside. While it was by no means a five star hotel, I kept quite warm all night. I even slept a bit, although my dreams were peculiar to say the least. I kept thinking a mountain lion or a bear would wander by and eat the moose—with me inside.

"Hey buddy, get up," said a voice, awaking me from my fitful and bloody slumber from inside the moose.

I had hoped perhaps the last two days were simply a dream—a nightmare to be precise. They weren't. I pulled myself out of the moose remains and squinted at the bright morning sunshine. I could see that the voice came from the policeman—the same one who I thought for sure had been killed by the moose. Somehow he had survived his ordeal.

"That's just sick," said another voice from behind him. It was Sammy, snuggled comfortably in a thick wool blanket.

The policeman draped a cozy blanket around me once I left the warmth of my moose cocoon. The officer looked at the moose, or at least what remained of it. He shook his head and said, "Comfy night? I suppose you didn't realize you were only a block from a gas station?" He kicked one of the gigantic moose legs. "And did you know we're outside of moose hunting season? I believe I'll have to fine you."

I stared at the policeman, wondering where my filet knife was, contemplating my next action. No, I had no desire to pick on an officer of the law. Besides, my adventure had run its course—time for someone else to go on a moose expedition. And I couldn't wait to eat something other than canned sauerkraut. Like maybe a thick, juicy burger—or perhaps a humongous moose burger. With lots of ketchup, because revenge is so very sweet.

History

A killer moose on the loose? Or maybe there are several of them? Killer *meese* on the lease? It remains to be seen. One thing's for sure: there are in fact rather large moose in captivity. Some weighing well over a ton.

As for them attacking humans? Well, that would be very rare indeed. They tend to do their own thing. The only contact they typically have with humans is when a car runs into them or they wander a little too close into town.

To me, while the story sounds fascinating, I find it hard to believe. Still, it seems plausible that a one-ton moose could go berserk and do some serious damage. There have been reported moose attacks throughout history. One in particular I found interesting was from Brent Olsen of Westford, Vermont. Apparently after napping in his car, he woke up to the sound of a deranged moose trying to crawl into the hood of his car. There's a YouTube video for proof—pretty crazy if you ask me.

Aside from the crazy moose in the world, it's still well documented about the size of the creatures. I don't know about you, but I wouldn't want to mess with an animal that weighed as much as your typical subcompact car. It's one thing to kick the tires on a Toyota Prius, but to kick the hooves of a moose towering over you? Not the best thing to do. Especially when the moose kicks back—or worse—bites back.

So how big can a moose get? Like I said, they have been reported to be over a ton. That's a lot of moose burgers. For example, Eric Arnette harvested a world-record monster moose in Alaska, in 2004, that had antlers seventy-five inches wide and 36 points. Or there's Jay, on a moose expedition in Russia near Alaska, who bagged a 2,300-pound moose. Very big indeed.

There's no doubt about whether monster moose exist. That part has been well documented. But are they monstrous in the sense of malicious attacks? In some cases, yes. But they typically do their own thing—and if you happen to get in the way, well… you better watch out. People do die from moose attacks, but it's mostly from a tragic car accident that gets in their way. Then again, you're more likely to have been killed by a deer while driving your car (no, not that the deer is driving your car, although that would probably cause even more fatalities).

*Artist's rendition of the Michigan Dogman,
a creature terrorizing those near the shores of
Lake Michigan—half-dog, half-man.*

CHAPTER 5

Michigan Dogman

Many presuppose that a Dogman is some fictitious, mutant, half-dog, half-man creature destined to live off table scraps in the shadowy gutters of your mind. I wish to God that were true—I could deal with a simple hallucination; unfortunately, it's far more than that. I'll never forget the chilling, yellow eyes staring at me and its yellow, jagged teeth, ready in an instant to rip my flesh apart and devour me whole. The Michigan Dogman is the real deal. I've seen it with my own eyes.

At the time, I lived at Ferris State University, over seven years to be exact, trying hard to complete a computer science major. All I needed was a deep passion for operating systems, hexadecimal math, data structures, assembler programming, and J-K flip-flops. Unfortunately, I had none of these things going for me. Hence I never graduated beyond an associate degree. Regardless, I became quite content with finding my real passion—living for the thrill of monster hunting.

Of course, there's not much money in finding monsters, let alone too many job openings on Monster job board (you would think there would be). The real gig that put food on my plate had me pouring beers at the local pub in downtown Manistee. As a bartender, I barely made minimum wage, but the tips covered the rest of what I needed, which typically wasn't much. Beer… food…monster hunting equipment…what else did one need?

One might think that monster hunting in Michigan would be pretty slow. After all, what kind of crazy creatures would hang out in the Midwest? Sloth monster, perhaps? Or maybe a cornfield monster? Surprisingly, there are tales of werewolves in Wisconsin, Wendigos in Minnesota, and of course the infamous Bigfoot, who seems to be everywhere nowadays. While these monsters are intriguing, and I had searched for them before, the creature near and dear to my heart is the Michigan Dogman. Sightings of the half-man, half-dog monster have occurred over the past few decades from Reed City to Big Rapids and now, thanks to me, in Manistee.

Hunting monsters can be a dangerous occupation, in more ways than you might imagine. This makes it difficult to find a brave soul to accompany me on my midnight expeditions. Rule number one deals with safety—always use the buddy system. That way, your odds are better in having at least someone survive the ordeal, if a monster goes postal. Finding someone to help with the hunting through the shadowy forest canopy is actually quite easy; the hard part is finding someone who takes the monster quest seriously. Derrick, my best friend since high school, tended to fit somewhere in between.

"So Billy, where're we going this time?" asked Derrick from the swiveling barstool while nursing a warm pint of Superior Stout. Apparently, he had consumed too many beers the night before and was more interested in the stale peanuts and popcorn.

"Not too far. Pretty close by," I said, swiping peanut shells off the table from the sloppy patron next to Derrick. I preferred having free popcorn, which cleaned up easier than the peanuts. Being that I didn't own the bar, my opinion meant little to nothing. I pulled out a map from the gas station down Main Street, pointing to the location where we would be hunting. "Manistee River State Game Area. I have a hunch the beast's there."

Normally, I wouldn't talk too much about my nocturnal escapades at the bar, for fear of scaring the locals or any tourists on their way to Mackinaw. Being that my boss wasn't in tonight I decided it acceptable. It also helped that nobody sat near us, except Jack Binge at the far end, plastered since ten a.m. beyond coherence and probably wouldn't notice a freight train rolling right through the bar.

"We've been there several times already," said Derrick shaking his head, hunched over, and staring into his mostly full glass. "There's nothing out there."

"Perhaps. But my sources say otherwise."

Derrick pushed his beer away and sat up. "Sources?"

"Old man Phillips and his wife. They live out there, close by at least. They were in two nights ago for their weekly pint of Miller Lite."

Derrick laughed, ending with a snort. "Like they would be reliable." He pointed to the end of the bar. "Mr. Binge would probably have more pertinent information."

To my surprise, Jack Binge looked up from the bar. He wiped the drool from his scruffy face and said in a slurry speech, "The Dogman is there." Several rounds of deep-seated wet coughing erupted from his lungs. Finally he added, "I seen it myself."

At first, I didn't know how to react. For months I'd been tending the bar, with Jack Binge at my side most evenings. On the weekends I'd be out hunting for creatures of the night, and never once did I think to check with Jack. He had lived in Manistee his entire life, so I was told.

"Such as?" I asked while meandering down the side of the bar, wiping the already clean faux granite top.

Jack tapped on his empty glass with his shaky index finger. That's when I laughed. "Yeah, right. You just want free beer."

"Suit yourself," he said, trying hard to clear the thick mucus from his throat, then settled back into his puddle of peanut shells and drool.

I stared at Jack, who comfortably rested on my bar with no care in the world, other than where his next beer might come from. What a miserable life. I wondered how he came into his drunken occupation. Perhaps his previous life weighed too heavily on his shoulders. Maybe something monstrous happened to him—like the Michigan Dogman?

Jack's wrinkled and weathered, brown face pulled up from the bar as he heard beer pouring from the tap. A wide yellow, toothy grin spread from ear to ear. "I knew you'd see it my way." He reached for the beer before I could finish dispensing. "The Dogman's for real." He gulped down half of the nearly full pint.

"Yeah, right," said Derrick who was still struggling to taste his own brew.

I leaned over the bar, grabbing Jack's glass as he set it down. Holding it tightly I said, "There's more beer for you if you're telling the truth. If you're pulling my leg, then you'll never get a beer from me again, paid or unpaid."

Jack effortlessly wrenched his beer free, then downing what remained in the glass. Jack's strength shocked me; pulling his beer away from my grip seemed to be effortless. He looked not a day over seventy, but I felt he had the power of someone in their twenties. He wiped his scruffy, week-old beard, then tapped on the glass. "It's empty."

I stood back from Jack and said, "Not until you start talking."

Jack stared at the tap for a moment, then his eyes glazed over, like he was gazing somewhere in the distance. "The Dogman lives. Or at least he did the last time I went out into that game area in Manistee River."

"And when was that?" I asked, still not sure where this would lead. For Jack it meant either more beer or no beer. I hoped he could fill me with truth, so I could fill him with beer.

"Years ago, maybe ten. I don't remember for sure—try to forget what happened out there, about the Dogman."

That intrigued me. Derrick, too, who had slid several barstools closer and actually took a sip of his beer. "Go on," I said, now leaning over the bar once again.

"I wasn't always like this, you know—a drunken old fool. I was just like the two of you, ready for any wild adventure that crossed my path. Even monster hunting. I heard you talking—I know what you do." Jack paused a moment, staring distantly for a moment, then added, "I used to do the same thing, until that night with the Dogman." Before I could react, he grabbed my wrist with a grip of steel and locked eyes with me in just as steely a gaze. He smiled, revealing his crooked, yellow teeth, and then let out a wickedly wet cough which sprayed my arm. "Be careful what you look for my friend. You just might find it."

I've often wondered what happens when you finally run into a monster. In just about all cases, a hunter is lucky if he at least finds some type of evidence—a footprint, a mysterious recording, or perhaps a picture. I had not heard of anyone coming face-to-face with a monster. Then again, that's probably because they never lived to tell about it. In Jack's case, he had apparently survived.

I jerked my arm away from Jack's grasp. Rubbing my wrist I said, "I know what I'm doing. Besides, it's not like you would ever run into a monster."

Jack snorted, then wiped the snot from his nose. "That's what I used to think. It was just a game to me, something to do on a Friday night instead of wasting away in a bar." He turned his eyes down to the empty pint and grunted. "Guess that's what I ended up doing anyway."

Without asking, I poured him another beer, topping mine off as well. "So what exactly happened?" I asked.

Derrick and I leaned closer to Jack, eager for his story to begin, which would probably start with, "It was a dark and stormy night…" It became dark all right, but not from his rendition of tromping around in the dead of night. The lights in the bar went out.

Silence filtered through the air, with only the red emergency exit sign above the front door illuminating the area, turning everything a shallow, crimson hue. Jack cut his sentence short, pausing only for a moment before whispering, "It's here… the Dogman."

I gasped at first, and then began fumbling around for a flashlight. "Why on earth would the Dogman show up here? I mean, I've been trying to find him for years. It's not like he would just appear on our doorstep."

A flare of light erupted from Jack's hand as he lit a homemade cigarette, which now dangled from his seriously chapped lips. He took a deep puff, and then let out a long exhale. He calmly said with a smile, "Like I was saying, Billy, be careful what you look for." Then a frantic pounding emanated from outside the front door, deafening rhythmic beats like syncopated thunder.

"What do we do?" asked Derrick, who now nervously gulped at his beer, as if it may be his last meal. Or maybe he wanted to use it as a sedative, to avoid the pain and savage attack of the Dogman. Was it really the Dogman?

Before I could respond to Derrick's question, the front door exploded, splintering across the room like a thousand jagged toothpicks. Luckily, most of the projectiles flew to the far end of the room, missing us entirely. Although, with what stood hulking in the doorway, being bombarded by tiny wooden shrapnel would have been a better end.

Light from the parking lot broke through the doorway, revealing a sharp silhouette of the monster. Its matted head and pointed ears bent down to look through the opening—the creature had to be over seven feet tall. I couldn't see its claws, but could hear them scraping along the door jam, then tapping, pausing for a moment, as if wondering what it should do next. I voted for eating Jack, who had to be nearly twice my size. Perhaps then the Dogman would get full and leave.

I reached for the baseball bat underneath the bar, slowly raising it above my head. The Dogman growled, which sounded something between a wolf and a grizzly bear—on steroids. It may have been a chuckle for all I know, laughing at my feeble attempt to protect myself. Probably like bringing a knife to a gun fight. Only the Dogman had knives, its steely claws still tapping on the door frame, and me with an oversized Louisville Slugger toothpick, which he may use to pick his teeth after devouring us.

Just when I thought it would attack, it raised an arm, motioning for us to come forward. The Dogman began to step back, still wanting us to come with him somewhere.

"I think it wants us to follow him," said Derrick in a shaky voice. He was obviously nervous. I was too. Jack seemed to be the only one not unnerved by the predicament.

"That's the last thing I'm gonna do," I said. "Probably just wants us closer to his den, or wherever the beast sleeps."

Jack stood up from his barstool with steely confidence. Even after several pints of beer, his motion was steady as a rock. He nodded to us briefly, all the while staring down the Dogman creature, like they were old foes from long ago. Which, according to Jack's earlier story, was in fact the case. Smiling, Jack said, "It's either stay here and get eaten, or follow him and maybe, just maybe, we have a chance to survive."

I kept my eyes on the Dogman as it backed into the parking lot. By all rights I should be wetting my pants and running like a sissy for the back door. However, something inside me, maybe a deep inner feeling beckoning to be a *real* monster hunter, saw this moment as an expression of freedom—to open up and explore that which is unknown. Or maybe I was just an idiot. Either way, I mustered every ounce of courage I could find, along with slamming a pint of beer, and moved toward the door. "Come on, let's do this."

Derrick stood there unmoving, other than his jaw swinging open. He shook his head and said, "Let's *do* this? What in God's name does *that* mean? This isn't some bingo parlor where you're risking a few bucks on a handful of chips and cards. That thing out there wants to *eat* us."

"Don't be too sure about that," interjected Jack, as he too started for the door. "If it wanted us for a snack, we'd already be carved up into at least a nine-course meal." He jabbed his finger lightly into Derrick's slender chest. "And you'd be the hors d'oeuvres."

Derrick remained stationary, watching as me and Jack walked toward the door. Finally, Derrick exhaled loudly and said, "Man, this is so stupid. Following him into his den is like committing suicide." He stood up and tried to shake the fear.

We followed the Dogman out of the parking lot and through several side streets, always keeping our distance, always staying in the shadows. A few times, we discussed running away, but the Dogman seemed to know our plan and would sprint at lightning speed towards our escape route. It was as if he could understand our language, and maybe even read our thoughts.

The full moon helped with visibility, but it also made the mood a little more freakish, like we were being lured by a menacing werewolf to our demise. Which we were. Regardless, I spent most of my time trying to come up with a way out of this. I no longer wanted the glory of being a diehard monster hunter, like the legendary Van Helsing. No, a gun would be nice right about now, one with a silver bullet. Yet would that work on the Dogman? What kind of bullet do you need for a Dogman? Or maybe just a poisonous chew toy would be enough. I seriously doubted that.

Within twenty minutes, we were past the city limits, shuffling along the ditch of U.S. Highway 31, dropping to the ground whenever a car drove by, which didn't occur too often. I don't know why we didn't flag down a car for help, but then I think that would be the last time we waved at anything. The Dogman was simply too quick for us to do anything, other than obey his commands to follow him and avoid being seen.

From Highway 31 we followed the Dogman down along County Road 55 until we reached the Bayous on the edge of the Manistee River State Game Area. After more than an hour of traveling through more ditches and bayous, we reached the Dogman's den. I could tell by the mounds and mounds of bones strewn about. Death and decay emanated from the bone piles, as well as from a dark hole at the side of a hill—no doubt the entrance to his humble and putrid-smelling monster den.

"Now what?" whispered Derrick, turning to me. "What's your plan?"

Plan. Yeah, that would be good to have. Except I didn't have one, other than maybe playing dead, but I'm pretty sure that would only make it easier for the Dogman to kill us. No, I think the best solution was to fight. I still had the baseball bat in my hand, surprised that the Dogman allowed me to keep it.

The Dogman pointed at the entrance to his den, motioning for us to enter. No way. That's the last place I wanted to visit. It probably has heads mounted on a wall above its fireplace, with three vacant spots waiting for us.

Just as I began to lift my arms and scream *kowabunga* and charge at the beast, Jack stepped forward and said, "Yes, I see. It's clear the creature is inviting us in to its lair, to learn from it, and understand who it is."

I rolled my eyes at Jack. "Are you nuts? I don't think this is some alien confrontation, where we're making first contact." I pointed to the discolored ivory bones littered about. "This thing eats creatures for a living—creatures like us. It doesn't sit around drinking tea and crumpets, wondering what the weather will be like, or if there's a good movie to watch on cable."

Jack ignored my comments, seeming almost delusional, sporting wide saucer-sized eyes, glazed over like two frosted donuts. "Nonsense. The Dogman is obviously a highly intelligent creature, able to thwart our attempts to discover it, perhaps even owning some type of cloaking device."

"Yeah," said Derrick enthusiastically, "Or maybe it can teleport to other dimensions," added Derrick, who obviously was buying into Jack's aberration.

"Shut it," I said to Derrick. Then I whispered, "We need to defend ourselves. It's three against one; the odds are in our favor." Of course, I knew how delusional that sounded. Three humans against a dark creature of the night, possibly immortal and highly intelligent, with claws and dagger-sharp teeth, not to mention lightning fast reflexes. We were doomed.

Jack continued with his deranged plan, but not before—what was that, a wink? Did Jack wink at me? He said, "There's no need to fight. We simply befriend the creature by accepting his invitation to his den." Jack bowed and began to walk forward. As he did so, he looked at me and mouthed the word, "run."

It happened in an instant. One second we were conversing about fighting or talking, the next second Jack was on the Dogman with lightning speed. Apparently, the old man had a few tricks up his sleeve after all. I could see two knives appearing from Jack's coat, twinkling in the moonlight as he began to slice and dice at the Dogman, who appeared to have been caught off guard.

"Run you fools!" yelled Jack, just as the Dogman began to fight back.

Derrick and I ran out of the boneyard, all the while hearing shrieks and curses from both Jack and the beastly Dogman. To this day, I'm not sure what happened to either, nor do I care. I made it out alive. Derrick too, and we never went back. As for Jack, well, I have a hunch he may have been just as much a monster as the Dogman. Regardless, he saved our lives that night. And for that I did what any good bartender would do—I named a drink after him. So come into my bar, the one I own now, and order one of my special drinks—the Dogman Jack. Just keep an eye on the front door, though—you never know who might show up.

History

The story about the Michigan Dogman has been around most notably for the past few decades, ever since a radio DJ from Michigan spoofed a song about a half-man, half-dog creature. He did this on April Fool's Day, so one might believe the whole idea of such a monster is a hoax. Yet if you look further into the mystery, you'll find the creature has been around for many years before.

The Ottawa and Chippewa tribes have known about the creature for centuries—a legend of a human hybrid that could shape shift into different animals, including a wolf.

As for the story above, it's based on several eyewitnesses who have run into the beast. One comes from a college student named John, living in Big Rapids. He reported that the Dogman creature apparently hangs out in a building around Reed City. John claims to have seen the beast himself. It appeared to be humanoid, six feet tall, and hunched over, with dark brown or black hair, and a definite canine-looking face with slanted yellow eyes. The creature chased them through some deserted buildings and then followed them at quick speed as they drove away.

In the fall of 1986, the Dogman was seen again, by a man named Ray in Manistee, Michigan. He had just left the army recruiting station where he worked, driving home late one night toward Ludington on the back roads around U.S. Highway 31. He noticed reflective eyes staring back at him from the ditch. He initially thought it to be a deer, but the eyes moved higher—much higher than where a deer would be. Then it leaped across the road in a single stride. It stood there on the opposite side of the road, with its yellow, slanted eyes staring back at him, and then disappeared into the night.

Finally, a man named Robert Fortney was gripped with fear when attacked by five dogs on the banks of the Muskegon River back in 1938, as recorded by Sheila Wissner in the *Record-Eagle* in April of 1987. Robert fired at the dogs, but his fear soon turned to terror as one of the dogs, "reared up on its hind legs and stared at Fortney with slanted, evil eyes and the hint of a grin."

There are many more stories about the Dogman in the Michigan area, as well as other areas of the country (not to mention the world). Perhaps there is a new species of half-man, half-dog? Or maybe just a hybrid of wolves? It's hard to tell. Maybe it's worth a trip to Michigan to do a little camping. Alone of course—much easier to catch a monster that way. Oh, and let me know if you run into the beast— that is, if you survive.

Spooky picture of a childlike creature, similar to the Mellon Head Creatures of Michigan.

CHAPTER 6

Mellon Head Creatures of Michigan

In October of 2001, two paranormal investigators disappeared in the woods near Saugatuck Dunes State Park, Michigan, while investigating stories involving the legendary Melon Head Creatures. The story below is based on the actual audio and video footage captured, which is all that remains of them and their investigation.

Video #01795-V
Allegan County Sheriff Archives.
October 13, Friday 2:32 p.m. 4 min. 27 sec.

The video begins with Matthew Bondalino filming Jason Milton as they drive toward the Allegan Woods—their first stop at Felt Mansion.

"Is that thing on?" asks Jason, pointing to the video camera.

"Uh-huh," replies Matt. "Filming the moment. Filming the now." The camera held by Matt turns to reveal himself and he says in a deep, newscaster voice, "On our way to Felt Mansion in search of the Melon Head Creatures. Film at eleven." Matt lets out a not so sinister laugh.

"Enough," says Jason. "There's probably nothing at the mansion. The bad stuff happened at the Junction Insane Asylum, but reports do come in from the woods around the area." Jason waves at the camera, attempting to bat it away. "Dude. Save some tape for the investigation."

"It's not tape, stupid. It's digital."

Jason is seen rolling his eyes. "Whatever. Memory then. Bits and Bytes. Save it for something important. Save the batteries, too."

"This is way important," Matt states as he pans out past Jason, focusing on the countryside as it streams by from the car, showing acres of already harvested farmland, barren with a dusty brown hue. "Got to document the trip. The adventure before the adventure. You know, what do they say? The adventure is not in arriving, but what happens along the way." The camera pans back to Jason as he's rolling his eyes again and shaking his head. Matt holds half a granola bar out at Jason like a microphone and says in a newscaster voice, "Tell me, Mr. Milton, what is it you're hunting for in the dark woods around Felt Mansion?"

Jason smirks, going along with the faux news reporting. He clears his throat and speaks in a serious tone, like an anchorman on the evening news. "The Mysterious Melon Heads of Michigan. Legend has it they once were children from an orphanage at Felt Mansion, back when it was a Seminary, where the sinister Dr. Crowe took them to the Junction Insane Asylum and conducted evil experiments." Jason releases a semi-demonic laugh.

Matt turns the camera to reveal the landscape out the front windshield. A white and black U.S. Highway 31 sign passes by, followed by a blue sign that reads, "Felt Mansion next exit." Matt whoops with excitement.

"Just a few more minutes and we'll be there." There's a slight pause before the camera pans to Jason. "So, do you think any of this stuff is real? I mean, come on, Melon Head Creatures?"

Jason sips from his super-sized diet cola, and then struggles to place it back in the cup holder on the center console of his parent's SUV, then cursing as some of the liquid spills. "Like any good monster story, you never know until you get there—until you're face to face with the beast." Jason takes his eyes off the road, long enough to stare into the camera and add, "That is, if you live to tell about it." Both exchange a series of overdramatic maniacal laughs.

Matt turns the camera to look out his side window, showing a sprawling, green landscape spotted with rising tombstones. An arching iron gateway approaches that reads, "Gibson Cemetery."

"Isn't this where Dr. Crowe's buried? Slow down a bit." Matt pans back and forth across the gravesites, with the setting sun casting tall, eerie shadows from the nearby pines. "We should go look for it."

Jason slows the car further. "Good idea. Maybe do some EVPs."* He turns the car around and heads for the entrance.

Video ends.

[*Electronic Voice Phenomenon]

Audio #01796-A
Allegan County Sheriff Archives.
October 13, Friday 2:47 p.m. 3 min. 42 sec.

Audio begins with Jason in calm, authoritative voice says, "EVP session 1, Gibson Cemetery. Outdoors with distant traffic and a steady wind blowing by." There is a slight pause. "This is Jason and Matt at Gibson Cemetery standing in front of Dr. Crowe's tombstone."

Matt asks, "Is there anyone here who would like to talk to us?" Silence follows.

"We mean no harm to you," states Jason in a continued calm, subdued voice. "Please give us a sign of your presence." More silence.

"Can't believe this is some wacky, mad scientist dude," says Matt. "Wonder if he really did it—you know, make all those Melon Head creatures, like some freaky psychotic Dr. Frankenstein."

"Only one way to find out," says Jason. He clears this throat and asks, "Did you create the Melon Head Monsters?" After a moment of silence, Jason adds, "Are you Dr. Crowe?"

"Duh, it's his tombstone idiot," Matt quickly replies.

"Shut up," says Jason. Silence follows. A low baritone chuckle erupts from Jason as he asks, "Are you related in any way to the infamous Victor Frankenstein?"

Something inaudible can be heard, a rumbling growl perhaps, followed by an abrupt high-pitched scream, then ending with an airy, raspy voice clearly stating, "dead time awaits you."

Video #01799-V
Allegan County Sheriff Archives.
October 13, Friday 5:36 p.m. 9 min. 13 sec.

Video begins with Jason and Matt rolling into the front turnaround of the Felt Mansion. The grand brick building looms before them, with its white-painted dentals and, just as white, dormers jutting from the high-pitched roof. Smooth Romanesque pillars stand tall at each side of the front entrance.

Jason pans across the front of the mansion and says, "This place is huge."

"Built back in 1928," says Matt, "for Dorr Felt and his wife. Although she didn't last long in it. Died six weeks after moving in."

"A curse of some sort, most likely for building on an Indian Burial mound," added Jason. "And Mr. Felt died a year later. Serious curse if you ask me."

"Or Melon Head Mounds. The dunes around the area might be filled with more than just sand." Jason and Matt walk up to the front door. Matt reaches out and wraps loudly. The door immediately swings open to reveal an elderly man dressed in a faded blue sweater and jeans, with his face sporting thick, bushy sideburns, white as ivory. His head is completely bald and a reddened, bulbous nose sprouts from his face. He might have been tall long ago, but age has sent him twisting forward with a prominent hunchback.

"Mr. Hale, I Presume? The caretaker?" says Jason as he extends a hand.

The caretaker ignores Jason's hand and simply nods slowly, yet firmly. He steps aside, waving them in.

"Thanks for letting us do a private tour of the place, Mr. Hale," says Matt. "You know, for paranormal evidence."

Again the caretaker simply responds with a slow nod. They walk into a large, open entryway, with a white-painted banister stretching up a long staircase. The caretaker stops and waves his hand forward again, signaling for Jason and Matt to investigate.

"I guess that's a green light for us," says Jason. The Caretaker nods once again, then turns and leaves through a side passageway.

The camera pans to Matt, who smiles and says, "There be a man of many words." They both laugh, and then Matt adds, "Come on. Let's get things setup."

Video Ends.

Video #01802-V
Allegan County Sheriff Archives.
October 13, Friday 6:49 p.m. 22 min. 7 sec.

Video starts with ghostly night vision on, panning across an unknown upstairs room in the mansion. After several minutes of Matt and Jason questioning the spirits, a loud thud emanates from somewhere below.

"What was that?" asks Matt as he moves the camera toward the floor.

"Beats me," replies Jason. "But I think we got them listening."

"Who's them? Mellon Heads?"

Jason is seen nodding his head. "Or maybe some other type of ghosts."

"Thank you for the sign," says Matt. "Can you do that again?" After a brief silence, a faint knocking sound can be heard in the distance.

"Thank you," replies Jason. He points down below. "I think we should head downstairs."

The camera shows them descending the main staircase in the darkness, lighted only by the Infra-red LEDs and the pale moonlight shining through the windows. Occasionally, Matt turns the camera behind them, pausing a moment as if something is following them.

"I bet the noise is the caretaker," says Jason, as he rounds the stairs and slowly moves toward the dining hall.

"Shouldn't be. He was supposed to leave the place to us for the night." The camera swivels around as another thumping sound erupts, this time coming from the back of the mansion.

Jason is seen immediately shifting his steps, heading down a hallway toward the source of the noise. The camera bounces along, following Jason as they dart into the kitchen. From the confines of the window, a bluish, glowing sphere, perhaps the size of a large head, floats briefly outside before a demonic high-pitched scream is heard, emanating from somewhere beyond the mansion.

The camera shakes violently and then abruptly stops.

Audio #01801-A
Allegan County Sheriff Archives.
October 13, Friday 7:17 p.m. 2 min. 3 sec.

Audio starts with loud shuffling noises heard, as Jason and Matt are on the run.

"Jason… here with Matt. Heading to the back of the mansion." Heavily breathing now. "We believe to have contacted one of the blue Melon Head Creatures. The thing… it screeched at us, then darted out into the woods." Slight pause, with frantic steps heard.

"It was right in that window," says Matt. He laughs briefly. "Dude, that thing was looking right at us through the window, and it's not like it was just standing there—the window is at least ten feet up from the ground!"

"But now it's gone," replies Jason. "Probably out into the woods."

"Yeah," says Matt. "Too bad we gotta go to the Junction Insane Asylum."

"Don't have to. Based on the evidence collected here, I think this is the place to be."

"But Junction should be the hot spot," says Matt.

"Should be, but isn't right now. Anyway, legend has it the Melon Heads are in the woods. And I think we just proved that."

"Not enough proof. Need to really dig in on this one. Should probably head into the woods. Camp there overnight like we planned." The wind picks up and howling can be heard in the distance, as if someone or something is shrieking gleefully.

Tape ends.

Video #01803-V
Allegan County Sheriff Archives.
October 13, Friday 8:37 p.m. 9 min. 56 sec.

Video, mounted firmly on a tripod, begins with Jason sitting at a small flickering campfire, with Matt walking away from the camera and sitting down next to Jason. Both are wearing white lab coats, making them glow somewhat in the silvery moonlight. A dome tent can be seen in the background.

"Do we have to document everything we do?" says Matt as he tears open an energy bar of some sort and begins nibbling on it. "What happens when I gotta take a leak?"

"Everything. Besides, you know as well as I do that's when the monsters or ghosts attack—when we're most vulnerable."

Matt laughs. "Yeah, you're right. It would be pretty hilarious to see the video of us running after a ghost with our pants down." Both of them laugh.

"Still, I'm not sure what we're up against with these Melon Head monsters. I mean, come on, these creatures used to be human, right? Terrorized and tortured by that evil Dr. Crowe, supposedly. Lots of bad experiments."

"Apparently, with a few that went way wrong—turning them into freakish beasts of the night."

"But they're only supposed to be like two or three feet tall. How bad can that be?" asks Jason.

"Ever seen the Holy Grail? That little cute and fluffy bunny—it did a number on King Arthur and his knights."

Jason rolls his eyes as he tosses the empty energy bar wrapper in the fire. "That was all fake. No such thing as demonic bunnies. Rabid yes, monstrous no."

"What about Harvey? You know, that seven-foot-tall imaginary rabbit that what's his name saw, Jimmy Stewart? Or the evil alien rabbit in *Donnie Darko*?" Matt tosses his wrapper in the fire. He nods his head and adds, "Yep. Rabbits can be ruthless. I'm sure of it."

Jason stares at Matt for a moment, no doubt wondering if he should continue with the demonic rabbit subject. Instead, he continues with the Melon Head discussion. "Supposedly the Melon Heads got the best of Dr. Crowe. They killed him, or some legends say they ate him. Hard to know, I suppose. Either way, the creatures were forced out of the asylum and into the woods."

"Wonder if we picked the right spot to camp. You know, if this is spook central or not."

"The motion sensors and cameras we setup at the perimeter will let us know," says Jason. "Although I'd rather not have any issues at base camp. No, the real action will probably be out in the woods somewhere." He chuckles and adds, "probably when we split up."

"Wish we didn't have to wear lab coats," says Matt as he straitens out the white elongated jacket. "Hard to keep warm in them."

"Doesn't matter," replies Jason. "It's supposed to help attract the Melon Heads, as if we are lab techs from the asylum."

Jason and Matt continue talking, with the crackling fire before them. In the distance, a small blue light can be seen, bobbing up and down only a few feet above the ground. A loud screech is heard, catching Jason and Matt's attention.

"What the—" says Jason as he stands up, looking toward the noise.

Matt jumps to his feet as well, then points. "Look—over there. A blue orb in the woods."

"Deeper into the woods," says Jason. "And it's probably not an orb. Probably one of those Melon Head Creatures."

"Luring us away from the safety of our campfire. But that's not gonna happen."

"Right," agrees Jason. "We'll just stay here and record—" Before Jason can finish his sentence, something large drops over the fire, extinguishing it. Screams from Jason and Matt can be heard in the darkness as the camera's tripod is knocked over.

Video ends.

Audio #01804-A
Allegan County Sheriff Archives.
October 13, Friday 10:02 p.m. 3 min. 02 sec.

Audio begins with heavy breathing. "Jason here... Not sure what's happening. Lost Matt..." Still breathing heavy, Jason can be heard shuffling his feet through the forest. "Ran away from... from whatever dropped on the campfire. Been running for quite some time. I don't know, maybe thirty minutes. I think I'm... lost."

Jason pauses, possibly looking around. He gasps, then says, "Oh Jeez. There it is again. That blue light. Maybe a Melon Head. Not sure what it is. Just need to keep away from it."

A scream can be heard far in the distance. "Jeez. What was that?" Jason yells, "Matt! That you?" More screaming. "Crap. I better go see."

Audio ends.

Video #01805-V
Allegan County Sheriff Archives.
October 13, Friday 9:57 p.m. 9 min. 11 sec.

Video begins with a dimly lit view of the dark moonlit woods. The camera swivels to reveal a petrified Matt, panting heavily and clearly distressed. "Matt here. Man, I don't know what happened. One minute we were... just sitting by the campfire. Then... man, I don't know. Something big dropped on us."

Matt, still motionless, pans out to the forest as he hears twigs snapping and dead leaves shuffle nearby. After a moment, he turns the camera back to himself. "We ran blindly. I lost Jason. Hope he's okay."

Matt's expression turns from bad to worse, with all color draining from his face as he looks away from the camera, into the woods. "Dear God... Oh Jeez. They're coming for me." He turns the camera around to reveal several blue figures about thirty yards away coming toward him. Now whimpering, Matt calls out quietly at first. "Jason? Need a little help here. Jason? Jason!"

As the Melon Head Creatures continue their advance, Matt emits a loud scream, broadcasting a terrifying echo throughout the dark damp woods. The Melon Head Creatures dart through the woods at lightning speed, showing up like blurring streaks of cobalt blue. Brief images of the creatures can be seen, showing their short, spindly blue bodies and their blue, elongated heads. Their expressions seem to possess anger or bitter hatred, or perhaps redemption, with their eyebrows pushed down around their clear, icy-blue eyes. Their mouths open to reveal yellowish, dagger-like teeth.

Video ends with Matt screaming violently as he drops the camera.

Video #01806-V
Allegan County Sheriff Archives.
October 14, Saturday 1:03 a.m. 4 min. 33 sec.

Video begins with a brief shot of the woods. Heavy breathing can be heard at first, then the camera swivels to reveal Jason sweating and heaving, obviously distressed with pools of tears and fear swimming in his eyes.

"Crap. Oh Jeez. I… just found Matt's camera. Reviewed his camera. It's… Jeez—I think they took him. Or, I don't know." Jason swings the camera out into the forest again, as if looking for something. "They're still out there, probably looking for me."

Camera is back on Jason. "I gotta find Matt and get us the hell out of here." He wipes snot from his nose and continues. "Just spent the past hour running, more like hiding, from these creatures. Can't seem to find my way out of the forest." He pans out to the woods again briefly, then back to him. "Man, this was such a stupid idea. I'm probably walking in circles. Should a brought a compass…"

A scream can be heard far in the distance. Jason points the camera into the woods. "Matt? That you?" More screaming, clearly male, and definitely freaked out.

The camera swings back onto Jason. "Man, I gotta… there's no choice. Gotta go get him. Jeez, this sucks."

The distant screaming continues as Jason shuts off the camera.

Video #01807-V
Allegan County Sheriff Archives.
October 14, Saturday 3:01 a.m. 47 min. 33 sec.

Video starts with Jason frantically running up one of several large sand dunes, looking at something on top. "Matt? Is that you?" After a struggle, Jason makes topside. He pans the camera down to reveal Matt, unconscious now, with his body roped and staked to the ground. His lab coat is torn to shreds, and deep, bloody scratches cover his face. "Matt — wake up!" Jason reaches out and slaps Matt.

Matt groggily rolls his head, slowly coming around. He finally opens his eyes and is immediately filled with terror. He screams, then yells, "Help me! Dear God! Get us out of here Jason!" Matt continues to struggle against the ropes, but cannot get free.

"Don't worry dude, I'll get you out of here." Jason sets the camera down showing the nearby woods. Tiny blue lights can be seen hovering in the distance.

"I feel like Lemuel Gulliver in Lilliput," says Matt off camera, trying to make light of the situation.

"As long as we get out of here before the Lilliputians arrive," says Jason. From the camera's view you can clearly see numerous Melon Head Creatures approaching from the forest, ascending the large sand dune.

"Oh God. No…" says Matt. "They're back!"

Jason and Matt are now screaming frantically as dozens of Melon Head Creatures climb the mound, all of which sport faces filled with anger and bitter hatred. The camera is kicked, shifting the view back to the mound to reveal Jason and Matt trying desperately to fend off the beasts, kicking and knocking them back down the mound like they were playing a sadistic king of the hill game. After several minutes of fighting, the Melon Head Creatures back off, drifting back into the woods.

Breathing heavily, Jason says, "I think we made it."

Exhausted, Matt wipes sweat from his forehead and says, "Yeah, we—"

Video ends with a low rumbling sound, then violent shaking as the ground beneath them swells. Dozens of pale blue hands reach up from within the mound, pulling Jason and Matt inside. The camera is knocked, rolling off the mound, tumbling part way down, before settling and revealing a dimly lit landscape of tall, shadowy pines and a full moon floating just above them. Muffled screams can be heard, but only for a moment; then all is silent.

Video ends.

History

The story is for the most part just that — a story. There are no records of any paranormal investigators disappearing. That, in my opinion, would have made headline news. Regardless, the underlying premise of the Melon Head Creatures of Michigan is filled with myth and legend. The question, however, stems more deeply into the filtering of fact from fiction.

It is claimed by several legends that the Melon Heads of Michigan started in the Felt Mansion (which was completed in 1928), of Laketown Township. They were originally children suffering from hydrocephalus, living at the Junction Insane

Asylum near the mansion. After dealing with abuse, both physical and emotional, the children turned into feral mutants and left the asylum for the surrounding forest. However, the Allegan County Historical Society indicates the asylum never existed, but at one point was a hospital. Regardless, teenagers from the area to this day recite the legends of the "Wobbleheads."

There are many versions of the legend, from the children once living in the mansion, retreating to underground caverns, or killing their doctor, Dr. Crowe, who abused them, forcing them to flee to the nearby forest. It has also been said they travel quickly, as fast as fifty miles per hour. Most of the sightings are along the Wisner and King Memorial roads near Chardon, Ohio, but also among the caves of the dunes near Saugatuck Michigan.

Yet with the many legends we hear, is it true? Chances are that this one remains among the books of fiction. Then again, why not take a trip to Laketown Township and find out for yourself? Just be careful camping on the dunes. I hear it may be a little unsettling.

Giant Turtle, supposedly haunting the shores of Lake Huron in and around Mackinac Island.

CHAPTER 7

Monster of Mackinac Island

… and the ancient, timeless beast known as Gitche Manitou, appeared from the depths of the Great Lake, awakening from its slumber, fathoms below, to feast upon the appointed sacrifice.

—Excerpt from the unearthed
Chronicles of the Anishinaabe (Ojibwe) Tribe

"Sam Johanson, *Detroit Free Press*," I relayed into my digital audio recorder while shifting away from others on the busy ferryboat. "Day one—Mackinac Island story." I stared across Lake Huron and continued. "The first thing I discovered while riding Shepler's ferry from Mackinaw City was that Mackinac Island is pronounced just like the city—Mackinaw." I smiled, remembering how the ticket taker promptly corrected my pronunciation error in routine fashion, as if she had done it a million times before—and probably had.

The second thing I learned, eventually, which intrigued me more (as my life ultimately depended on it), involved the island's dark and mysterious past, cloaking it in a supernatural mist worthy of any nightmarish tale spawned by the likes of Stephen King, H.P. Lovecraft, or Dean Koontz. At times, I felt my life on the island surreal, spiraling into some Lovecraftian adventure with monsters beyond imagination, ready and eager to devour my flesh and soul in some slow and baneful way. Or maybe I had hallucinated everything, stemming from an ill-fated confrontation with spoiled fudge. Yeah, right. Mackinac Island Fudge would never spoil.

Don't get me wrong—the people and places of Mackinac Island are amazing. Friendly and courteous—above and beyond your normal neighborly way. To me, it encompassed the perfect getaway, which is what I suspect most of the 15,000 tourists who visit the island each day in the summer believe. I, on the other hand, have discovered a darker, more sinister past—one the locals are not willing to talk about, and try even harder to forget. Yet the pages of history, when blemished by evil, never die, which is more than I can say for myself.

The ferry ride took only a few short minutes and in no time I found myself at the Grand Hotel, off Grand Avenue, checking in. The time on the island would be good for me, or so I thought. Not so much of a vacation, for I had work to do. Harold Loffameyer, my pudgy, middle-aged boss at the *Detroit Free Press,* told me to do a cover story on Mackinac Island. I pleaded with him, trying hard to talk him out of it. Being single and in my twenties, and with an excellent physique (if I

do say so myself), I had no grand intentions to sloth around in museums, lounge dreamily on covered porches, or stare endlessly at interesting geological formations created from a previous ice age. No, the only thing that interested me was the nightlife—from dusk to dawn.

"Sammy, do you think great stories come from big events?" said Harold on many occurrences. "No," he would always reply before I could answer. "Great stories come from big writers of small events." I was no Hemingway, that's for sure. I wouldn't be publishing the next great American novel anytime soon. Regardless, taking a break from the downtown Detroit action couldn't hurt, right? I couldn't have been farther from the truth.

"Tourist?" asked the woman at the hotel front desk from behind her oversized, thick-rimmed glasses and an undersized toothpick smile. She was a plump lady of somewhere south of forty, with her auburn hair bundled up in a bouffant—like she'd just stepped off the ferry from the 1960s.

I began shaking my head and was about to spout off about being a fancy journalist from Detroit, but decided against it. The element of surprise might benefit me, preventing the locals from spoon feeding me all the standard niceties and touristic qualities of the land. "Yes," I replied with a polite smile. "In from Detroit."

Her smile stretched wider but remained thin as I handed her my Id and credit card. "Ah, Mr. Johansen. You're practically a local. Probably know all the stories from the island."

"Actually, I've never been here before."

She swiped my card, all the while donning her plastic grin and staring at me. No—perhaps through me, like I wasn't there. "Well, then you're in for a treat. Lots of stories on the island to be told, don't you know." As she handed back my credit card she leaned forward, her faux smile drooping somewhat and asked in a more serious tone, "Do you believe in ghosts? Monsters even?"

I couldn't tell if she was asking seriously. Still, her question intrigued me. *Why would she ask me that?* A tourist trap most likely, set to snare your typical spooked-out ghost-hunting wannabe. As for me, the only thing supernatural I believed in had to do with the mysterious disappearing sock from my dryer. Two socks in, one sock out. Or maybe the poltergeist-like activities of where I *thought* my car keys should be, or in some cases the location of my car when parking at the Target Superstore. Regardless, I played along with her line, nodding and matching her smile evenly.

Finally, a warm, genuine smile sprung from her face, like gloomy clouds parting. "Well then, you're in for a treat," she repeated, now beaming. "Lots of things that go bump in the night here, don't you know." She leaned closer and whispered, "Even in the hotel. But I'm not supposed to talk about them." Then loudly thumped on the counter three times and said, "Bump-bump-bump!" She paused a moment, then slowly waved the key card to my room. "Especially in room 209."

I believed I was just handed my golden ticket. Perhaps this sluggish weekend getaway wouldn't be so dull and dreary. If anything, sleeping in a haunted hotel room might put an interesting slant on my article. Too bad I didn't believe in any of that paranormal crap.

The remainder of my first day on Mackinac Island was uneventful. I settled in to my proposed second-floor spooky room without so much as a "boo," or raspy, whispering voice behind my ear. At one point, however, I did hear voices, but after a minute of sleuthing I debunked it as conversations from the front porch down below. As I peered out my window at the people conversing, I did see something peculiar: an elderly man, dressed in blue-striped flannel pajamas (thoroughly matted and wrinkled), even with the afternoon sun high above. He sat in a rocking chair motionless, turned away from everyone. I could see his toothless and puckered face casting no shine, a powdery, dull white, yet his bulbous nose was bright red. His eyes were cloudy and distant, and his thinning, long, gray hair was fluttering in the gentle breeze. He wore no expression, sitting there like an elderly zombie on vacation. Perhaps he had a long morning visiting the museum, or spent too much time wandering among the many shops off Huron Street.

I wondered for a moment about my own life—where it was going to be exact. Or, for that matter, where it wasn't going. Would I be stuck as a stuffy journalist in Detroit the rest of my life, never making it big as a writer by penning that ultimate American novel? I shook my head, turning away from the tattered old man in the rocking chair, thinking, *I could be him in a few years*. Yet...could it be that the old man was happy? I looked back again. No, while his lips were thin and unmoving, his placid eyes had much sorrow pooling in them, the kind you get from a life wrenched and twisted with misery and misfortune.

I looked beyond the old zombie man, up at the heated sun. Perhaps the old man simply needed a friend, someone to chat with? Yes, and he might have some terrific stories to tell. I smiled at the thought of sitting with him over a few beers, mounting enough tidbits of information to finish my article. I turned to look at the old man, to flag him down and perhaps join him, but he had vanished. No one sat in the rocking chair, yet it continued to sway back and forth in ghostly fashion.

I spent the rest of the day gathering details about the island, meandering from street to street, store to store, trying my best to be tourist-like, all neighborly and friendly. That was another hang up—I never came across as the most sociable man. That didn't help my ability to sponge stories from people. But I loved writing, getting such an ethereal high as the words flowed from brain to fingers to keyboard to page. Sometimes when I wrote, I felt like Buddha experiencing enlightenment, or maybe Saint Francis with an epiphany. Regardless of my sacred and esoteric state of mind, I had a story to complete, which wouldn't happen in a vacuum, so on I went door-to-door, like some traveling journalistic salesman.

While I did capture some decent information about the island, it was by far too dry—bland at best. Just standard things you'd find in a local history book or chamber of commerce website. Still, the details might come in handy. On the bright side, through my wandering I discovered something most amazing: Mackinac Island fudge. After sampling several pieces, I made the wise decision to buy a pound of the heavenly goodness and made a pact with myself to devour it back at the hotel. Yes, it would make the perfect meal, and I would become a true tourist, or Fudgie as they're known among the locals.

Later that night, I woke from my bed with a terrible thirst, as if all the water in my body had evaporated. Springing from my bed, I stumbled through the darkness toward the bathroom to consume numerous glasses of water, hoping to loosen my tongue from the roof of my mouth.

Fumbling for the light, I glanced at the clock on the bedside table. It glowed in phosphorus red 01:53. I looked to the window, which was open (and which I clearly recall being shut prior to my fudge slumber). It was black as asphalt outside, with the exception of a few flickering street lights, so I assumed it was either the middle of the night, or an unannounced solar eclipse had occurred.

I also surmised that the fudge had gotten the best of me, sinking me into the bed and inducing an intense chocolate-sugar coma that had lasted several hours. As such, I no longer felt like sleeping. With the odor of fudge still lingering in the air, I decided it would be a perfect opportunity to explore the hotel, at least until I felt the sprinkle of sleep from the sandman arrive, which no doubt would occur sometime around 7 a.m. when everyone else would be waking up. I gathered pen and paper, slithering past the remaining slab of fudge on my nightstand, and headed for the lobby.

Still dealing with the aftereffects of the fudge, I shuffled slowly to a vacant lobby chair, rubbing my eyes and squinting from the intense light. Perhaps jotting down a few sentences within the confines of a comfy hotel chair might do me some good. It would either spark my interest, in which case more sentences would flow, or it would put me to sleep. Neither happened, for just as I dropped my hand to the paper, the crazy old man in flannel pajamas appeared.

While I could clearly see him shuffle across the lobby, shifting his thin and frail body toward the front door, he seemed altogether distant, as if gazing far beyond the hotel into some other universe. The old man stopped for nothing, looked at nothing, seeming to be hell-bent on exiting the hotel. The lights in the lobby flickered and buzzed as he shuffled by. I turned to look for the front desk attendant, but she had disappeared. Alone in the lobby, I swiveled around to see the old man—still zombie like—pushing through the front door with ease. Bright light from the street lampposts shined through the doorway creating a shimmering silhouette of the old man, and wind rushed in, making his spindly hair flow backward like gray streamers. It didn't take me long to know what to do next. After all, I had the blood of a journalist in me—I followed action through thick and thin, penning stories for all to read. This, my friend, might be just the mother of all stories for me. Instinctively, I sprang from my chair and followed the crazy old man out the door.

The chilling air of the witching hour pressed against my face, making my skin tingle and my teeth chatter. While I knew it would be cold, this seemed beyond that. I could see the frosty breath of the barefoot old man as he continued forward, determined to complete some unknown task outside, or arriving at an unknown destination, all the while spouting his lifeless and catatonic face.

The old man picked up his pace at the side of the hotel, nearly sprinting. I stepped up my advancement, making sure not to lose sight of him. As I turned the corner of the hotel, I could see a carriage in the distance, complete with horses and driver. The old man headed toward it, never missing a beat. A silver bell hung off the carriage to the left of the driver and jingled heavily, slicing through the silent night, sending dagger-like sound bites echoing across the street. As I neared the carriage, tingling pulses of energy shot through my body. Looking closer, I could see the driver cloaked and hooded, but where a face should be, I saw only a dark void. As for the horses, they seemed normal—large and muscular with silky black coats shimmering in the moonlight. They snorted occasionally, sending bouts of breath spiraling into the misty air. But the eyes—that's where things seemed altogether wrong. They were like large, crimson-colored rubies, like round pools of blood ready to burst at any moment. I turned away, shuddering at the sight.

Fear had consumed me—something I had never experienced before—not at this level. I feared things like death, or losing a loved one, or perhaps the daunting task of finding a mate for marriage. But fear of zombies, vampires, werewolves, or any other creature of the night? Hardly. They did not exist, or so I thought. Yet there I stood, staring at demon horses, the black rider of death, and the drooling zombie man as he climbed unknowingly into the dark carriage of morbid oblivion.

So I did what any normal, living human would do. I turned and ran. *This can't be happening!* I thought several times as I hurriedly darted back to the safety of the hotel. I could hear the carriage rolling off into the quiet darkness, with the demon horses neighing shrieking fits of triumph, suitable for the devilish likes of Nosferatu, Prince Vladmir, or Beelzebub.

Stumbling head-first into the lobby, I turned and slammed the door shut, hoping and praying the demon carriage wouldn't burst through and take me to the Netherworld. I paused a moment to suck in air deeply, my heart racing, sweat beading across my forehead, my back wedged hard against the front door. Looking around the lobby, I saw no one. Then again, I didn't expect to see much at around two a.m. I looked at my watch, confused. It read just after four in the morning.

Where did the time go? I shook off the lapse in time and headed for the front desk. Once again, the area was vacant, other than faint music coming from somewhere back in the nearby office.

Flustered, I reached for the bell on the desk, tapping it loudly once. Waiting only a few seconds, I reached again for the bell, this time pounding it repeatedly, like I was beating a bongo. Still no response. Angrily, I stomped around the counter toward the back room. The music got louder as I approached and I could hear either Smashing Pumpkins, or maybe Nine Inch Nails. At that moment I began to feel that oppressive fear covering me. An enormous pressure landing on my shoulders, like an elephant had just sat on me. I stumbled backward, nearly falling, turning at the last moment to see the old man staring at me. His face was devoid of all expression. Only he didn't have eyes—the sockets were filled with squirming maggots and dripping, oozing pus. This same infestation littered his mouth, nose, and ears. The sight had me gagging and sucking air. I dropped to the ground into a secure fetal position, praying to God, Allah, and Buddha, hoping at least one of them would be listening.

I woke in the morning, my vision pierced and flashing by the bright sunlight. Panic hit immediately, as I recalled my horrific night terror, but quickly calmed once I recognized the safety of my own hotel room. *Had it just been a dream?* I nodded, hoping to convince myself as I rolled out of bed. I smiled. *Yes, it had to be a dream.* I laughed, thinking how great it would have been for a story, other than the part where I would most likely have been devoured by the maggots of the old zombie man. Perhaps someday it would be the makings of a great horror novel, but for now, *just the facts ma'am.*

Breakfast in the hotel restaurant went down easier than I expected, even with my nightmarish sleep. Eggs with sausage and biscuit—what better morning meal is there? Coffee for beverage—a sincere necessity. What better way to start the day? I had brought pen and paper to the table, just in case inspiration found me—which it did. Of course, none of it had anything to do with reality. No, my thoughts were focused on my recent nightmare, with words of terror flying speedily across the paper. The creativity bubbling in my cerebral cortex pleased me; the fabrication of amazing scenes and dialog were all too fluid, all stemming from somewhere between the Great Ether and the spot between my ears.

Or maybe not? While I wrote the words off as mere illusive conjectures, a tiny part nestled somewhere in my brain still believed they were true. That spot fully embraced the awareness of the previous night, noting it as reality. That's when I looked up and noticed the police approaching.

Having finished the majority of my breakfast, I quietly left the table and followed the police toward the front desk. I grabbed a newspaper along the way and sat down at a nearby chair in the lobby, pretending to read. From what I could decipher, the two uniformed officers talking to the lady at the front desk were concerned about something of importance. *Duh*. If the police were called, something "not good" had occurred. The look on the woman at the front desk told everything—she was freaked out, her eyes the size of tennis balls and her arms gyrating around in a nervous fashion. She did not look like a happy camper.

After several minutes of listening and questioning and note taking, the police calmly left with a polite nod and smile. Being the journalist that I was, it didn't take long for me to discover the facts. Within seconds, I befriended the front desk attendant (who actually had been working the nightshift) and had absorbed the gist of the details.

"What's wrong?" asked the front desk attendant. The badge on her tan, polyester uniform read Candi, making me think about the famous island fudge I'd eaten the night before and wondering if she enjoyed the dessert as well.

"Huh?" I replied, not realizing she had been staring at my freaked-out expression. It alarmed me that the police had shown up—which could be related to a missing person, most notably the old man from my dream the night before. *Or was it a dream?*

"You look like you've seen a ghost," replied Candi, as she forced a smile and wiped her watery eyes. The events of the morning had not been kind to her; with lack of sleep, she struggled with her composure and ability to extend that Midwestern friendliness.

I nodded. "I guess so. The police—they're looking for someone? An old man?"

Candi's eyes widened. "Yes. Why, have you seen him?" She threw her hands to her side and exhaled deeply. "I don't know why I have this job. Can't seem to do anything right. And now… gone! An old man has been missing for days!"

I relaxed a little, knowing the person I saw had been shuffling around alive just last night. "Sorry, Candi. I was just… I thought maybe I knew the old man. Odd guy, long wavy gray hair, dressed in flannel pajamas, and walking through the lobby all zombie-like. But that was last night."

Candi lowered her jaw. "Wavy hair? Blue pajamas, striped?"

Now my eyes bulged, and my jaw dropped. "Uhm, yes. But—"

"You saw him last night? Impossible. His son called this morning and said he hasn't been heard from since last Tuesday. The other weird thing was his room—it had been locked since this morning, with the deadbolt. Maintenance man broke in, thinking the old guy was in there sleeping, or maybe dead, but he found nothing."

"I saw the old man yesterday—on the porch in a rocking chair just staring out at the lake."

Candi stared at me a moment longer, then straightened her blouse. "I think I had better contact the police again."

The last thing I wanted was to waste precious time pestered by police questions. I had an island to discover and write about. Then again, this could be another part of the story I needed. Reluctantly I agreed and said I'd be in my room if the police needed me.

As I walked away from the front desk toward my room, I could tell the incident had shaken her, her face washed white as snow. I felt no different. Something odd had occurred and I was determined to find out more. My plan involved first freshening up, then heading to the local library to do some research on missing persons, as well as any other tidbits of information about legends and myths. There was always the possibility this was bigger than just one missing person. Unfortunately, fate had other ideas for me. As I entered my room, that same sickening fear smothered my awareness.

With fear mounting deep inside, I forced myself into the room, which seemed unusually chilly. *Had I left the air conditioner on? In October?* My frosty breath wafted into the air. While everything in the room looked just as I had left it—bed with sheets pulled back and the quilt on the floor, disheveled pile of clothes from the night before scattered across the chair and desk—the air wreaked of terror. The only item out of place was the window—it had been opened and a chilling breeze blew through. I forced a smile, knowing that this most likely explained my cold sensation. Nothing spooky or terrifying—just an open window. Or so I thought. As I closed the window, a hand reached in, threatening to pull me out to the street below.

My first instinct involved screaming, which I did quite nicely—a high-pitched squeal any elementary school girl would be proud of. Next, I put my free hand on the window sill to keep from falling out. I then yanked backward, which proved to be a good idea, keeping me safe and inside the room. It also proved bad, for the thing that held me down had come into the room as well—on top of me.

Once more I was confronted with the old man, still donning his pajamas, which were now filthy and seriously ragged, with long wavy hair, and a zombie gaze from his black tar-pit eyes, which looked much better than the maggot infestation from before. He effortlessly pinned me to the floor. Breathing heavily, with horrid bad breath, the old zombie man began drooling on me, causing thick oozing pus to drip on my chest. *Yuk.*

"Get off me!" I yelled, but to no avail. He had to be half my weight, yet he seemed immovable.

"Be warned!" said the old man in a raspy, crackling voice. "Island of the dead! Island of the dead!" he added. With his hands gripping my shoulders, he shook me until I thought my collar bone would splinter. With one final shake he commanded, "Leave us!"

That's when the maggots and millipedes appeared again, starting to slowly drop from his mouth. I closed my eyes, but could still feel the creepy crawlers dropping onto my face and chest—which made opening my mouth to scream difficult. Just when I thought my end was near, being suffocated by squirming slimy things, the old man vanished, leaving me to scream in solitude. I lay there a moment, panting heavily. *Was this another dream?*

I sat up abruptly, checking for any leftover maggots squirming across my face. No wormy creatures could be found. Everything seemed normal, other than the window still being open—which I wisely chose to leave that way. There's no reason to repeat the last few minutes. Sweat beaded my forehead as I crawled into bed and lay down, shivering from the recent fright. The room then began to spin as darkness swept in, with sleep soon smothering my awareness.

By the time I awoke from my near catatonic state, the sun had already peaked, signaling noon. Obscure thoughts littered my head as I tried to focus on what had happened, and what to do next. *Call the police?* No, they would be contacting me if they needed me. *Talk to the front desk again?* No, that would only freak Candi out further. With my hunger returning, I eyed up the remaining fudge on the bedside table. There was only a pound or two left—what harm could that be? But didn't I only buy a pound? Regardless, I nibbled on the chocolate delight, and then frantically stuffed the rest in my mouth, like I hadn't eaten in a week.

The events (or dreams perhaps) of the last twenty-four hours had me feeling like it was time to leave the island. Yet I had a story to do, a job to finish. Heading back to Detroit empty handed would be the last thing I would do. Then again, staying on this island might *be* the last thing. Reluctantly, I chose to stay, intrigued by the mystery unfolding around me.

Like any good journalist I headed for the public library, just off Huron Street, to roll up my sleeves and get my homework done. There had to be something in the island's past that tied to the recent events plaguing me.

The library was deserted, other than the librarian. The woman standing before me sported classic Gothic-style garb, dressed in black from head to foot, and included a murky, dark pearl, nose ring and matching eyebrow ring. She wore her jet black hair short, and the top jutted out in spiked, frazzled-hair fashion.

"Can I help you?" she said while chomping on gum with a wide, open mouth. *Gum? In a library?*

"Yes, I'm here to do some research."

"About what?" she asked, now snapping her gum loudly, as if annoyed.

"The island. I'm doing a—" I paused, not wanting to reveal my identity as a journalist and taint the information I might receive. I needed to remain undercover, at least a little while longer. "A book report," I finished.

She flashed her eyes up and down my body, no doubt surmising I may be a bit too old for book reports. "Yeah, right," she finally said, rolling her eyes. "Whatever." She pointed to the computers near the front, then at the reference section to the

side, and went on to explain about the microfiche in the back room. I nodded and made my way to the nearest computer.

As the sun set, darkening the light through the nearby windows, I had sleuthed through nearly everything I could find. The best information had come from the microfiche—more specifically the archives of the local newspaper. It can easily take hours or even days to sift through a large volume of microfiche, but I had it down to a system. I could make my eyes sort of unfocused and just absorb the details flying by on the microfiche, then stop as I saw something I needed whizzing by.

There were clearly some interesting things going on around this island. Sure, there were the occasional hauntings, like that of the Bailey House, or from the Mission House, and of course Fort Mackinac. However what interested me most had to do with what the maggot-infested old man said to me, that Mackinac could be an *island of the dead.* As far as I could tell, things were quite lively around here, and everyone seemed pleasant and happy. *But perhaps too pleasant and happy?*

As it turns out, the old man appeared to be right. Mackinac Island had been inhabited by the Native Americans for centuries. In fact, it had been a sacred place to them, and you guessed it—a burial ground. Apparently there were scores of bodies buried on the island. More importantly, they had been moved from place to place, or at least most of them.

For me, that solved the mystery. The old man was just some ghostly figure of my mind, a by-product of my freakish imagination. Yet perhaps some part of it was real, a wink from the spirit world, trying to send a spooky message about all the restless spirits. The little I knew about ghost hunting told me this just might explain everything. If anything, it at least would make for a great story back in Detroit. Front page perhaps? Smiling with confidence that my story had finally come to me, I reached to turn off the microfiche display, only to find all the lights going out.

At first I was annoyed. *How could that Goth librarian wannabe do such a thing?* Although it could have been some automatic motion sensing switch? I waved my hands, hoping for the lighting to return, but it did not. I sighed deeply, frustrated with the sudden darkness. As I lifted myself out of the chair, I could feel a chilling breeze rush by. *Had the air conditioner kicked in?* Perhaps, as it did feel frightfully cold. Or maybe it was—

It's difficult to describe with words what happened next. A deep, guttural moan bellowed from somewhere in the darkness, not too far away, like a released demon from the depths of hell—all raspy and rumbly. Electrified zapping noises followed, springing to life an energized silhouette across the doorway of the room. The old man appeared, hunched over and breathing heavily. His hands, elongated like thin alien fingers, wrapped around the door jam. "Leave!" the old man yelled with his crackling throaty voice. "Leave!" he repeated.

"Gladly," I replied, trying to control the fear mounting inside. "But you're in the way." I tried my best to remain calm, although my trembling body said otherwise.

Then, with photon-like speed, the old man darted around the room, like an over-caffeinated marathon runner. He continued to moan the word "leave" as he shifted simultaneously from one location to the next, before abruptly halting in front of me.

In a soft, gurgling voice, he whispered one last time, "leave." It seemed more like an implored suggestion, from deep inside one's heart, like his life — or perhaps his death — depended on it.

"Gladly," I repeated, trying hard to ignore his gaze, to avoid looking at the rotting maggots inside his head.

The old man, seeming to grasp my defiance to his demand, reached and tightly grabbed my arm. At that moment visions of ghouls and other nightmarish things from beyond danced about.

A panoramic view of the island stretched out across my vision, from a bird's eye view, or that of a helicopter. The hotels, shops, houses, and forest in the distance could clearly be seen. The sight was spectacular, that is until the zombies appeared. Starting in the forest, several slithered out from behind trees. Soon, however, the walking dead poured out from the ground, into the streets, each with their glossy-eyed gaze, staring into nothing, or perhaps something beyond — to the deeper parts of the lake.

The dead walked across Mackinac Island, dozens, then hundreds, and finally thousands, all headed for the southern shore. The lifeless army of the decayed eventually reached the shoreline, and then abruptly turned and marched down Huron Street. This continued for some time, until they turned and went north along Lake Shore Drive. Thousands of zombie creatures, all lined up in unified fashion like a morbid parade of death, marching toward… I knew where they were going — I could feel it as the dark frosty thought entered my body… Arch Rock.

I didn't understand the criticality of Arch Rock; all I could sense was its power and darkness that brewed a terror that filled me with death and wretchedness. I noticed something else meandering through the legion of zombies — a black carriage with even blacker horses streamed down Huron Street, also headed for Arch Rock no doubt. The carriage with its ringing bell seemed familiar, and I quickly remembered where I'd seen it before — it was the same one that the old man had ridden in the night before. *Or had he? Wasn't that just a dream? Or had I been seeing the future?* Hardly — unless this too might just have been a dream, yet it felt much too real.

I found my view narrowing, flowing downward like a swooping bird, finally resting near the Arch Rock. The horse and carriage had arrived, with the moon above full; however, it did little to brighten the mood. Everything went silent. I could feel the air electrify, sending tingling and zapping sensations throughout my body. Then a deep feeling of emptiness and solitude devoured my awareness, leaving me with a sadness unbound. Next, I found myself moving closer to the carriage,

enough to see a coffin in the back made of plain unfinished oak, void of any ornate carvings. I had no desire to open the casket, yet I knew it must be done, as the hooded driver looked to me, and then pointed toward the coffin. I also understood who inhabited the box—something that sent shivers deep inside. Without warning, the casket door flew open, exposing the decayed remains of… me.

I awoke in my hotel room with beads of sweating across my face, and my shirt drenched. *Another dream?* I thought as I studied the clock at my bedside table. For a minute I thought it read 6:66, but shook my head and looked again, this time it read 6:06 p.m. I reached for my phone to check the date. Thankfully it was still the same day, just a few hours later. Still, how had I gotten back to my room from the library?

Questions rolled through my head like a quickly spreading fog, then developed into a throbbing headache that I could not shake. *A good dinner and a good drink should fix things, but definitely no fudge.* I massaged my temples, hoping to rub away the migraine. I washed my face, changed my shirt, and headed for the restaurant.

The burger and fries had to be the best I'd ever eaten, or maybe I was just that hungry. Either way, I felt content. After a couple cold beers, the world seemed to be a better place, or at least not so morbid and fearful. Yet the recent dream still haunted my thoughts. Whenever my mind wandered too far, it ended up back at Arch Rock, like I… should be there… now. No matter how hard I tried, visions of Arch Rock kept appearing. Soon my relaxed atmosphere disappeared, transformed into a world filled full of anger and bitterness.

"You look miserable," said a voice from behind. It was Candi from the front desk. "White as a ghost, too."

"It's nothing," I said, annoyed at her interference. It wasn't her business to worry about me.

"Is everything all right?"

"Does everything look all right?" I snapped. I didn't need her or anyone around right now. I just needed to… sleep. Rest would do me some good. And maybe more fudge.

"I see…" said Candi, who I expected to be taken back by my rudeness. Instead a smile developed, slightly mischievous? "Perhaps a little rest will help."

Before I could respond in some rude and condescending way, she promptly left.

"Fine," I yelled while pounding my fist into the table, then grabbing my head because of the migraine that still pounded. Everyone in the restaurant stopped talking and eating, trying their best to ignore me. I slammed my fist back into the table, just to make a point. *I'm here and I'm angry, okay?* I thought to myself, but wanted nothing more than to scream. *What was getting into me?*

After a moment of staring defiantly at several patrons in the restaurant, I decided that sleep would be the best thing, that and another pound of fudge. With several samples of chocolate delight in hand from the hotel gift shop, I headed for my room.

While my sleep seemed peaceful (probably the most serene in a long time), I felt a chilling breeze flow across my body, eventually bringing me back to consciousness. As my teeth chattered from the cold, I looked at the bedside clock—two a.m. Looking around the room, I immediately saw the source of the frigid air. Once again the window had been opened. While my initial instinct was to roll out of bed and close the window, I thought back to the dream (*or reality?*) with the old man grabbing me from outside the window. No, I left the window alone and instead went for an extra blanket in the closet.

While I stood there in my striped flannel pajamas (*Flannel pajamas? Since when did I wear them?*), testing the silkiness of the extra bed sheet, I could hear a lone bell ringing from somewhere outside my window—far outside my window. Immediate visions of carriages, corpses, and coffins filled my mind, but not in any horrific way that would send one screaming for safer realms. It felt to me altogether… peaceful.

Of course, a part of me shrieked in horror, trying hard to awaken my senses, to remind me that dead things as such were always bad. Yet most of my brain felt comfortably numb, consoled, and mesmerized by the obvious morbidity. Eventually my mind gave in, allowing all things dark and dreary to win. I soon found myself shuffling in a zombie-waltz toward the hotel front door.

The following paragraphs are excerpts from Samuel Johansen's digital audio recorder, found near the crime scene, and is all that remains. The investigation by police is still pending further leads and evidence.

"Sammy here. It's the middle of the morning. This is crazy, but I'm heading out of the hotel. Not sure why, but it's something I have to do…something I've needed to do all my life."

There's a slight pause.

"This is so cool…so exciting. I feel like I've finally been awakened to the truth."

Slight pause again, then it continues.

"The bells are ringing in the background, or maybe…my head."

A door can be heard closing in the background.

"Heading to the lobby now. Anxious for the carriage. It's so peaceful. Honestly, I've never felt more alive."

Steady footsteps can be heard.

"Oh, hi Candi. Wonderful evening."

"Yes it is. Your carriage awaits you Mr. Johansen."

Sounds of the hotel front door opening can be heard, then more footsteps. Neighing of horses rumble in the background as a door (carriage?) squeaks open.

A door closes and Samuel says, "Driver, to Arch Rock if you will!"

The clomping of horses' feet echo in the background as Samuel mumbles incoherently from time to time, noting such things as zombies, ghouls, and demons. Some words are clear on the recording, which he repeats numerous times: "Gitche Manitou!" followed by, "The beast awaits!"

Sounds of the horses subside as the carriage door squeaks open.

"At last! Arch Rock and its sacrifice!"

Samuel can be heard walking for several minutes, sometimes stumbling, as if climbing over rocks and through bushes. Then Samuel can be heard laughing hysterically, as other footsteps can be heard around him. The rattling of chains echo into the otherwise silent night.

"Chains! Sacrifice! Gitche Manitou will be pleased!"

Silence follows for several minutes. At this point something large can be heard crashing from the splashing waves below, slithering and scraping up the shoreline, getting louder as it approaches Arch Rock. At this point it appears as though Samuel, who seemed initially mentally imbalanced, awakens to the reality—he can be heard screaming in terror. "No! What am I doing here? No!"

The slithering and scraping from some monstrous creature stops. Samuel's screaming has stopped, left only to deep heavy breathing.

"This... can't... be. It's humongous. A... giant turtle creature..." He laughs hysterically once again, perhaps falling back into his deranged demeanor. "Ha— hungry Mr. Turtle? Time to feed? I am your sacrifice Gitche Manitou!" More heavy breathing, followed by a bellowing roar from the giant turtle that even Godzilla would be proud of.

Samuel can be heard laughing in a crazed banter as the turtle-like monster Gitche Manitou emanates another earth shattering roar. Chains can be heard snapping like twigs, Samuel's laugh is cut short, followed by horrendous chomping and crunching, and then all goes silent.

History

Giant man-eating turtles? Human sacrifices? Could this possibly be true? Probably not. Then again, what sort of world would materialize if your entire island was essentially a giant Native American burial ground, being bothered by tens of thousands of tourists each year? That might be enough to raise the dead, let alone a carnivorous mega-turtle.

Arch Rock of Mackinac Island, where legends indicate human sacrifices may have been carried out.

It's no secret that Mackinac Island has a supernatural ambiance surrounding it. Many year round residents have experienced a paranormal presence. Perhaps that's because of the century's-old inhabitance by the Native Americans, as far back as the 700s A.D. and prior to the European exploration around 900 A.D. The earliest known inhabitants are the Anishinaabe (Ojibwa) tribe, who considered this island a sacred place, home to the Gitche Manitou, or Great Spirit. It also was the final resting place for their tribal chiefs, with many of them buried on the island.

As for other reasons the island may contain a supernatural presence, there have been countless lives lost. Such as the following:

- Nearby, on Bois Blanc Island, several British soldiers in the 1800s were killed, slaughtered by the Native Americans.
- In Fort Mackinac, children supposedly haunt the officers' hill quarters. Also, skeletons were found within a "Black Hole" of the guardhouse. And a phantom piper and his music can be seen and heard along the nearby North Sally port.
- More skeletons have been found at the Grand Hotel when the foundation was dug.
- Apparently, the little horse corral was at the site of the first Post Cemetery, and not all of the bodies were transplanted when the cemetery moved to its current location.
- When soldiers made a garden in Marquette Park, it was reported that over 1,000 human remains were found.
- The Mission House is also filled with the paranormal. In particular, countless Native American children had been reported to be housed down in the basement after being diagnosed with the sickly Tuberculosis (TB). Many accounts by state employees have been reported of ghostly children in the basement.
- At the north side of the island, during the war of 1812, the English slaughtered seventy-five Native American men. Since then, people living on the island claim to see Native American men running through the woods at night.
- Post Cemetery is known to have a woman weeping near a set of graves close to the left corner of the cemetery. Also, those hiking along the Rifle Range trail can still hear the sound of bullets firing.

As you can imagine, there are numerous situations in which the paranormal may interact with the normal. And, in some cases, the supernatural may cross over into our natural world. But giant man-eating turtles? Who knows? To be safe, I would think twice about waltzing into the streets of Mackinac Island during the witching hour, or strolling into the woods near Arch Rock alone at night. Then again, what better way to discover the unknown? Perhaps bring some fudge with you—I hear giant turtles love fudge.

CHAPTER 8
Bessie
The Lake Monster

Artist's rendition of a lake monster, similar to the one lurking beneath the waves of Lake Erie.

Some people joke about monsters, turning back a page or two to their childhoods, thinking about the creatures from underneath their beds, or the demons in the depths of their closets, or maybe the memories of a dark slithering something in their basements. As for my monsters, they are rooted in the not-too-distant past. My monsters are all too real, having nothing to do with the creatures of the night, foraging about in one's humble abode—but everything to do with silvery serpents of the deep. While I survived my confrontation with Bessie, others have not. This is my story—more of a warning from the personal nightmare I lived, meant for those foolish enough to venture forth into the depths of Lake Erie at night. Boaters beware…

The weekend at the lake had been planned for weeks, starting first and foremost with a boat—as big as I could find. Thankfully, my parents had an old, eighteen-foot Boston Whaler parked in the Huron Marina. They agreed to let me borrow it, but only if returned in one piece, and sparkling clean from bow to stern. No problem there. As for friends, that would be easy. I would invite my best friend and current Bowling Green State University buddy, Francis, along with two sorority girls, Jill and Meredith, who we'd met last weekend at the local watering hole, the Knucklehead Saloon. Yes, my friend Francis had kind of a girly name. He preferred that over Frank, which he felt was a bit too burly for him, even though his thick, stocky frame could easily have him passing as a seasoned Canadian lumberjack.

As for Jill and Meredith, they were serious girls, their brains were sharp. They were tall and had dark hair, with even darker skin, dazzling hazel eyes, and each with a face like Aphrodite. With beauty and brains they were perfect...except they were a bit stuck on themselves.

"Oh my God!" said Meredith as she stared in a mirror while sitting in the front of the boat. "This mist and splashing waves is making me a mess!"

Jill pulled the mirror from Meredith and looked at herself. "Oh my God! You're so right." She sighed deeply, disgusted. "Why is it so humid?!"

"Beer anyone?" asked Francis as he flipped open the cooler. We had just stocked it with several cases of Leinenkuegel's Berryweis—a personal favorite of mine, having grown up in Chippewa Falls, Wisconsin, where it's brewed.

"Beer me," I said with my hand outstretched. Francis tossed one in my direction. "Just one though, since I gotta drive."

"Works for me," said Francis. "More for the rest of us!" He cracked open a beer and chugged heartily. The girls each had one as well, but daintily sipped them. I started the boat engine and navigated the marina for open water. Our trip had finally begun. Little did I know it would be the last—for some of us.

The afternoon proved to be amazing. Perfect weather, with little wind and no rain, removed us from the monotonous ways of our normal lives, replaced by activities of serious awesomeness. We started with water skiing, of which the girls showed off their physical abilities by eventually dropping a ski. Francis and I were not so athletic. Our one-skiing attempts lasted all of five seconds, ending with a face-plant in the water, which felt like slamming into a sidewalk—while running at thirty miles per hour.

Tubing was next, which fared much better than the skiing for Francis and me. We worked the wake like pro snowboarders on an Olympic pike. As for Jill and Meredith, they were not so lucky. They spent more time in the water than on the tube.

With the water sports ending, we concentrated on our next task—fishing. The weather had turned a bit sour, with the wind and waves coming in, making things a bit choppy. Clouds were forming high above, but the weather reported nothing but scattered showers tonight.

"Hand me another piece of bait," said Francis as he set his rod and reel up against the side of the boat.

"A little help," said Jill as she dangled her empty hook in front of Francis, all the while flashing her hazel eyes.

As I handed Francis two pieces of bait, Jill screamed with joy. "Caught something!"

Her rod curled sharply toward the waves. "Hold onto the rod!" I yelled. It looked like she might let it go. "Reel it in," I added.

"It must be huge!" Meredith squealed. However, as Jill continued to reel, it became apparent her catch was nothing to write home about.

As the fish surfaced, Jill yanked, sending her backward into the boat, along with the tiny fish. It was the smallest Lake Trout I had ever seen, ten inches at best. Jill quickly stood up, pulling on her line with the fish on the end. "Take my picture! Take my picture!"

"Really?" I blurted. Seeing her excitement, I obliged. After the picture, I began unhooking the fish to toss it back.

"We're keeping it, right?" asked Jill.

"Uhm, no," I replied. "Too small."

"Can't we keep it for a while?" she asked, flashing her eyes and gleaming.

I smiled back, shaking my head. "Can't keep it in the boat if it's not legal size. Sorry." I tossed the fish back into the water, and then reached for more bait. "But I'm sure there's bigger fish out there to keep and eat." What I didn't realize was who would be eating who in the end. Bessie lurked out there somewhere beyond the boat, ready and waiting for the right moment no doubt.

We caught several decent-sized fish, all lake trout, which would make for a great meal later in the evening. As we finished the last of the bait, Francis caught something big—really big.

"Whoa," said Francis as his line zipped out and his rod bent nearly into the water. "This thing is huge."

"Steady, nice and easy, "I said, as I went over to watch. The line darted left and right, like the fish was circling the boat. It seemed to take hours for Francis to bring the big fish in. Just as it reached the surface, however, something even bigger swooped from below and attacked his fish. Everyone screamed and backed away from the side of the boat. That pulled Francis' fish up and into the boat as well—at least what was left of it.

"Dude, something huge chomped on your fish," I said while investigating the bite mark, which extended entirely across the fish just behind the gills.

"It bit my fish like it was bait," said Francis, dismayed.

I punched Francis lightly and said, "Looks like we have Jaws out there." We all laughed at the statement, but underneath we began to wonder. *What kind of beast* was *out there?*

As the sun dropped to the horizon, we filleted the fish we caught, tossing the entrails in the water, and settled in for a terrific feast of trout, potato salad, pretzels, and beer. It may not have been the most romantic meal, but the setting sun helped compensate.

With the sun fully set, Francis decided to tell a few ghost stories, illuminated by the dim boat lights and a Coleman lantern. In lieu of a campfire, we circled around the beer cooler, placing the lantern atop. The wind had subsided, leaving the boat to a gentle rocking. We were about ten miles out from land, and with a quick weather check I knew we'd be good for the night, as the sky above filled with twinkling stars.

Francis' first ghost story fell short of anything terrifying, telling the tale of a couple and their run-in with a classic women-in-white, on a deserted highway after their car had broken down. Still, the yarn brought Jill closer to Francis and Meredith nearer to me.

By his third story, and fourth beer, the girls were on edge. More importantly they were tightly clinging to us. Nothing better than a horror story to get a girl close. Francis went on about the Victorian mansion, haunted by the family done in by an axe murderer—based on a true story, of course.

When he got to the part where the ghost, carrying a phantom axe, walked down the hallway to the terrified babysitter and kids hiding in the bedroom closet, and with the ghost's axe thumping the floorboards as it walked, Francis reached out with his free hand and thumped on the cooler. He paused for a moment, the lantern light streaming up to accentuate flickering shadows on his face in ghoulish fashion; then he raised his hand and screamed, like the axe-wielding ghost, readying himself to strike.

Everyone, including myself, matched Francis' scream, flopping back to the deck in a brief moment of horror. Francis' gut-wrenching laugh echoed across the water while the rest of us remained silent. Eventually, all of us laughed, enjoying his spooky epic tale. Our humor soon abated, however, as the thumping began once again.

"Knock it off, Francis," I said.

"What?" he asked. "It's not me."

"Okay, girls; joke's over," I said turning to them.

Jill, who had apparently been enjoying the beer all too much, was clearly drunk. In a slurried voice she replied, "Ish notsh me." Standing up, she stumbled forward, holding her hands up. "Look aht me. My handsh up shere." She giggled briefly, and then teetered backward, hitting the side of the boat and plunging into the water.

"Jill!" screamed Meredith, who had not been drinking as much, but was still experiencing some serious effects of the beer. She laughed and added, "It's not a good time to go swimming!" More giggling.

"Quiet!" I yelled. The thumping had stopped—only the splashing of light waves against the boat could be heard. "Francis, throw the life preserver over." I turned to peer over the side of the boat and listened. There were no signs of splashing or laughing. I feared the worst for Jill. Then, after several long seconds, she surfaced, giggling like nothing had happened.

"This is great!" said Jill as she began swimming around the boat. "You guys should come in!"

"Sounds like a plan!" yelled Francis while pulling off his shirt. But that was the last we heard from Jill.

We saw her swim around the bow, laughing all the while, then nothing. No scream, no big splash, just silence.

"Jill?" I asked after a moment. "You there?"

More silence.

"I'll jump in and look for her," said Francis, who had stripped down to his shorts. He slipped into the water while I grabbed the spot light to search.

"Jill!" I yelled, followed by shouts from the others.

Francis spent his time diving into the water, yet each time coming up alone. He slammed his fists into the water, frustrated. Then, far into the distance, splashing could be heard.

"Jill!" yelled Francis.

I flashed the spotlight in the vicinity of the noise, and after a few seconds saw that it was in fact Jill—or at least what was left of her.

Francis screamed—he could see that the remains of Jill were being propelled toward us, with Francis directly in the way. As Jill came closer, we could see something in the water—something gigantic.

Within seconds the monster was upon us, overrunning Francis in the water, and then slamming with full fury into the side of our boat. The hull ached and moaned, with a definite crunching and splintering sound emanating from somewhere underneath the deck. The boat itself heaved, sending Meredith and myself nearly in the water. Then, silence.

"Francis?" I yelled while pulling myself up from the deck. The boat had a serious list, and water could be heard trickling in down below.

"What do we do!" screamed Meredith. The smartness from her brains seemed to have diminished to almost nothing, leaving her with the inability to think straight. Instead, she focused on her primordial screaming.

"Relax!" I yelled to her, grabbing her shoulders. "We'll get the life raft. We'll be fine." I was lying of course. I had no idea if we'd make it another minute, what with some monster lurking below. Jill was gone, followed now by Francis. We were most certainly next on the meal plan of the creature from the depths.

I pulled out the life raft and activated the inflation device. Within a minute we had a fully functional raft. I also punched in our coordinates and distress signal for the coast guard to hopefully find us. In the meantime, however, we had more important things to deal with—like surviving an attack from some hungry sea monster wannabe.

Figuring we might be out in the raft for hours, if not days, I threw the cooler in. It had mostly beer, but also a few sandwiches. Good enough to get by. I also tossed in a lantern, flare gun, and ammo. Once situated, I would send out a flare every hour for those nearby to rescue us. Of course, nobody was probably around—it was two o'clock in the morning and miles from anywhere. No, we were probably stuck there for the night. That is if we could survive the lake monster's appetite.

I never saw myself as an amazing hero kind of guy. Yet in the face of danger, I apparently could remain calm and stay in control. Sure, Jill and Francis had no doubt perished. But I would protect Meredith to the end. Or at least that was the plan. It would have worked, if it weren't for Meredith getting all psychotic.

It really didn't have much to do with her. I felt like going crazy myself. You see, I believe the lake monster had a huge amount of intelligence, for it seemed to be playing with us, making us go crazy. If it wanted to, we would have been monster munchies within seconds. But no, it swam around the raft, just out of site, splashing and churning in the deep waters when we least expected it.

After about an hour of constant panic, Meredith screamed frantically. "I can't take this!" She tried to roll out of the raft and into the water, the whole time yelling, "Eat me! Eat me!"

I held onto her as best I could. "Calm down. Hang in there!" Unfortunately, her fingernails got the best of me, digging deep into my arms. I screamed at the pain, loosening my grip and sending her into the depths of Lake Erie.

It seemed like the lake monster had been waiting for this moment, for within seconds, it appeared only a few yards away. The head was immense, the size of a car—much bigger than the raft. Its mouth opened to reveal a set of dagger sharp teeth. But what I remembered most about the creature was its eyes—brown and murky, like pools of quicksand luring you into its bite.

Instinctively, I reached for the flare gun, aiming shakily at the beast. The flare shot, sending a glowing red ember at the monster's flattened snout. It shrieked in pain, a deafening sound I will never forget. Then it dove, no doubt to feast on Meredith. As it went under, I could see its snakelike body slithering for what seemed like eternity. At the end of the creature, the tail splashed, tearing into the life raft and sending me into the water. I would have surely drowned, and thought for sure to be consumed next by the beast. My only hope for survival was the floating cooler, still filled with beer and sandwiches. I clung to it, hoping and praying the monster had gone.

Thankfully, it never returned.

By sunrise, I could hear a helicopter overhead, soon followed by a large vessel—the Coast Guard. There was nothing left of my parents' boat, nor any of my friends. While I tried my best to explain to authorities exactly what had happened, nobody would believe me.

As the weeks and months trudge on, I wonder myself what had happened. Regardless, I now stay far away from large bodies of water. I have stopped swimming in pools and even avoid taking baths. I mean, why take the risk?

History

Is there a monster lurking in the depths of Lake Erie? Or perhaps Lake Huron? With such large bodies of water, one might think there's an easy chance for strange creatures, such as the infamous Bessie, swimming in the shadows. There have been many such reports.

In some cases the lake monster has been seen twenty- to thirty-feet long, gray or black colored, sometimes as long as fifty feet. It can have brown viciously sparkling eyes and large fins—or possibly a dog-shaped head with a pointy tail.

A 65-year-old resident of Ontario claims to have seen the serpent lake monster. While enjoying a morning ride, his boat "hit something big," then started to rock. He held the side rail for safety. The water by the boat began to boil, as if something was going to surface. It surfaced, then left peacefully. This was one of many sightings by the Ontario man.

For centuries, the Native American Ojibwas tribe has claimed there's a giant reptile living near the mouth of Serpent River. According to Mrs. Louis Day, a splendid storyteller, there is a legend of Ojibwas boys. In their thirteenth summer, they would journey from their village of Spragge to the Sacred Spot, currently known as Herman's Point off the big lake. With fasting, they would wait for visions of spirits to reveal their destiny as a great medicine man or hunter. One such boy came to the Sacred Spot with a small blanket from his mother to protect him from the rain. After several days, the boy become discouraged with no spirits appearing and he was ready to go home. His mother, however, had other ideas. She impressed upon her child that if he stayed a little longer, the spirits would eventually reveal themselves. The next day, the mother returned to check on her boy at the Sacred Spot, but he was nowhere to be found, although the blanket she had given him was hanging from a tree. She and the people of the village searched for the boy, but could not find him. Weeks later, some hunters from the village saw a "great commotion" in the waters of the great lake. Then, a giant creature with great horns arose from the depths, with the mother's young boy riding atop. After that, terror gripped Spragge village. People began to disappear, swimmers in particular, with strange sounds echoing through the night.

Mrs. Day remembers being awakened at night by the peculiar noises. Eventually, she had to move. To this day, she claims the terror stems from the serpent of the great lake.

Many legends indicate there's not one lake monster, but many. Reports include:

- From Lake Huron, Ontario, Canada: several generations of a family report seeing many "huge monstrous snakes in the lake."
- One other report is from a grandfather, who was an eyewitness to the snakes of the lake. The grandfather said the creature's head was three feet long and two feet wide, with its neck out of the water by at least ten feet. This has been reported near Sauble Beach, as well as by Chiefs Point.
- Near Port Elgin, someone has reported finding a huge snake skin, over twenty feet long and two feet wide, along the dock area.
- A large number of snakes were reported in 1975, near Kincardine, Ontario, Canada—although some believe this may have been due to a group of relic seals.

- In 1989, near the Goderich area, two "long log-like" creatures were observed.

It seems that the lake monsters are typically reported in large bodies of water, similar to the one found at Lock Ness in Scotland. They reportedly have similar characteristics; Bessie of Lake Erie is no different. Or even Pressie of Lake Superior. With such large volumes of water and abundant sources of food, there's no doubt there is a potential for monsters of the deep. And while many have claimed to see some type of creature, no real evidence has of yet to be provided. Still, the elements for a large creature like Bessie to exist do make it plausible. Perhaps someone in the near future will provide real evidence—a video or photograph? Maybe that someone will be you? Just try to use a boat that's bigger than the monster.

Storm Hags tormenting the body and soul of an ill-fated sailor from Lake Erie.

CHAPTER 9

The Storm Hag of Lake Erie

Come into the water, love, dance beneath the waves, where
dwell the bones of sailor-lads, inside my saffron cave.
—Excerpt from the *Legends of the Storm Hag*

My dwelling place is fathoms deep and most might say quite miserable. Not for the likes of my kind, mind you. It is the creatures called men who cringe at the thought of my lair. Men—land dwellers by right—feebly attempt to circumvent the space above my domain. I scoff at their endeavor, knowing well enough they should not venture too far from shore. Yet they do—and that is when we feed.

We are an ancient race called Storm Hags, or Water Spirits. Many of my sisters travel the larger bodies of water—the endless seas. As for me, well, I chose a different path, one full of quietness and solitude. That is, of course, until I grow hungry. Angry too—which is what happened with the ship called the *Clevco*.

I remember all the vessels I've taken to my lair, far beneath the churning waters of Lake Erie. I keep them in my graveyard of ships, like game mounted on a human hunter's wall (so I've heard). They are well concealed, mind you, hidden in my saffron cave. The *Clevco* I recall the most vividly—its shipmen were the most difficult to lure—and in turn my greatest prize. Yet like all my human prey, I prevailed.

It was late December in the early 1940s, as humans count. As for me, time is an illusion, for I am a creature eternal, or at least my species has never experienced aging and death. I have lived longer than I can remember—most certainly well over a thousand years.

As I have said, the *Clevco* was a special prize to me. It left the human town of Toledo, on its way east. The winter months were the worst times for ships to travel in my lake, what with frigid temperatures and steely ice; this made shipmen make poor decisions—which bade well for my thirst of souls.

The *Clevco* ran into tough waters near the coast of Cleveland, having to be escorted by another ship, smaller, named the *Admiral*. As I watched from below, following their progress, I smiled devilishly, knowing I soon would be getting two ships in the night.

The *Admiral* and its crew would be consumed first. Not, however, before having a little enjoyment. You see, catching souls has less to do with the outcome,

and more about the adventure. The victims must *know* they are stalked, and to eventually find themselves confronting their fate of an untimely death. Why would I do such a thing? It simply makes the soul taste that much better.

While the weather across Lake Erie had become bitter and choppy, with a moderate northerly wind briskly blowing through, the waves were by no means treacherous. Balmy for the likes of the *Admiral's* crew—I could see in their eyes as I peered through the moonlit darkness that the watery routes of Lake Erie were no stranger to them. They fared the ebb and flow of surf like few others. What a shame to snatch their souls, no doubt from a place they felt most comfortable. Yet this game of soul-catching was beyond me—the spirit of my quest transcended any thoughts or actions of my own—I must do that which I am made to do.

As with the powers bestowed upon my kind, I summoned a small storm, local to their route. As I have indicated, my soul catching must first induce a fertile adventure. It must be filled with conflict, trauma, false security, and ultimately a clear recognition of their own demise. A squall builds conflict and concern, which, in turn, makes the crewmen stand true to their merit and conviction. Then, just as the storm dissipates, and all seems well, I strike.

I increased the storm's intensity, playing with their wills. Ending their lives with a storm would be much too easy. I had command of the water, like Poseidon himself, though not at his depth. I was a lesser god, but still fit for condemning the likes of any mortal.

As my self-created gale subsided, I began the next phase of my malicious plot. I began swimming near the surface, easily within view—even in the dark, cloud-filled sky. Soon panic sets in on the crewmen, like all other times, on all the other ships I have consumed. Their steely actions become loosened, slackened by their fear of the unknown. Yet, I am not that unfamiliar to them; my name and deeds have been propagated from ship to ship, lake to lake, ocean to ocean. Any seasoned seafaring mortal knew of us—we were the mighty, soul-snatching Sea Hags. All bent to our needs; all were devoured by our hunger.

They soon began to see my green skin and long spindly arms, and I flashed my yellow glowing eyes. That's when their fear is set, replacing the worldly knowledge of ships they were so accustomed to. Mistakes begin to be made, ropes are let loose accidentally, routes are miscalculated—that is when I release my full fury.

The storm had depleted in strength, to the point where clouds had vanished and the moon began to spread light across the ship and waves. At least for the *Admiral* and its crew. As for the *Clevco*, still tied to the tugboat *Admiral*, I had set forth a fog to entrap them, keeping them distant and aloof of the impending *Admiral's* demise. With the hearts of the *Admiral's* crewmen comforted, I begin my song, which lures them beneath the waves, a swan song impossible to resist, tempting them to an illusively better world. Then, with their souls mesmerized and trembling with ecstasy, and with a clear, star-filled sky, I command the waves to part, sending the *Admiral* swirling and sinking below to my domain.

The whirlpool does not happen swiftly, for what sort of sport would that be? No, the *Admiral* descends slowly, for each and every crewman to gaze into my eyes — to see my electrified power and fiery fury. Then, one by one, they meet the gnashing of my dagger teeth, biting deep into their flesh. They know, however, that the devouring of their bodies is the least of their concerns. There are worse fates for man. They know my prize does not stem from flesh and bones, but from their very soul.

Within minutes (although for those of the crew it seemed no doubt like an eternity) the *Admiral* was no more. I had prevailed once again — like so many other times before. But even with my centuries of skill and knowledge, I had made one minuscule mistake. The *Admiral*, though a small ship and an easy challenge, had been tied to a larger, more potent, vessel — the *Clevco*. While one would think it obvious to sever the rope holding one to the other, I could not. No matter how much power I commanded of the lake beneath and the storms above, I could not remove the bond between the two ships. It held like an oath, a commandment of souls between the two separate vessels.

The consequences were horrific. I was forced to rip the souls of one crew, while retaining the lives of others. I enjoyed the adventure of tormenting them, like my other sister Storm Hags, but this was too much even for me. I had to act promptly, to either relinquish my stash of souls from the *Admiral*, or bring the crew of the *Clevco* to a speedy demise. Being a Storm Hag, born of creatures worse than demons, I readily chose the latter.

It took time, mind you, which led into my adventure of soul stealing. Hours went by with the crew of the *Clevco* awake and alert to the swelling lake around them (yes, I spent time conjuring squalls to incite concern — and to occasionally create heroes, mind you). Their will was played hard throughout the night, ever pondering if they'd live to see the light of day. They did, but not by the hand of my goodwill. And that is why the *Clevco* stands out as one of the greatest ships I have ever caught.

While I may be one of the lesser gods, with the ability to command only a localized fury of water storms, I recognize that there are other gods, some possibly stronger than myself. I spend a great deal of time ensuring I do not meet the likes of them. Yet no matter how much focus I give on this prevention, it happened in the case of the *Clevco*.

I do not know what god helped them out, but it was far stronger than me — at least initially. I fabricated storm after storm, tossing them upon the floundering

Clevco, with my usual abatement in between, then swarming close to show my demon-spawned green skin, sharp dagger teeth, and yellow illuminating eyes. Yet nothing would bend the will of the crewmen. No sooner had I opened the water to swallow them whole and ready myself to consume their flesh and souls, when a power unknown to me would ascend, forcing me to abandon my approach.

Dawn came and went as I battled endlessly with this unknown force—a god beyond my knowledge and comprehension. To this day I know not which god I battled. Still, I would not give up—the challenge only fueled my task, pushing me beyond my normal, watery, cat-and-mouse game that I played. Countless times I sank the mighty *Clevco*, yet every time it prevailed, forced up from the depths of my cave and ship cemetery by some shining and fathomless power. An illuminating energy pulled the vessel each time from its grave, sending it back atop the waves, more buoyant than before.

Just as I was to relinquish my attack, giving up all hope—a stroke of luck sprouted. I say "luck" because there was nothing done on my part. On my last bout, the crew seemed to have given up all hope, relaxing their grip on the watery reality around them. I could feel it, their souls' power departing from their bodies. I smiled a yellow dagger tooth grin—soon the passion encapsulated within their hearts would be mine.

This time, the vessel sank and did not return. I devoured their souls one by one, basking in the fear and flesh of their watery grave. The ship splintered into tiny fragments, becoming a ghostly field of shadows from its once mighty size. I beamed a greater jagged grin as the crew's last mate succumbed to my wrath, and I watched the grand *Clevco*—blood, bones, and wood—settle on the lake floor, nestled up against the other prize ships in my collection. The battle was over and I, once again, had won.

Some say a wicked beast such as the likes of me has no soul. I refute such a statement. There are plenty of souls within the walls of my fiendish flesh—all captured of my own heartless doing.

Ye who embark across the mighty Lake Erie, beware. Whether it be sailing, swimming, or perhaps innocently prancing across the shoreline—all take heed to my warning. You have entered my dominion and are subject to my stinging power and torturous watery ways. You may pay the ultimate price—one that will relinquish your soul. Yet what harm could that be? You weren't using it anyway, right?

So, in the calm after a storm, on whatever waterway you navigate, as the waves subside and the sun's rays poke through the dissipating clouds, listen for the song of my sisters:

"Come into the water, love,
beneath the waves,
Where dwell the bones of sailor-lads,
Inside my saffron cave."

If you listen intently, and do as we say, your end will be quick. If not, may the god you worship provide a swift and painless death, for we will certainly not.

History

The prior story is for the most part based on the numerous shipwrecks around the Great Lakes. This includes the mysterious disappearance of the *Clevco,* in December of 1942.

The *Clevco*, an oil tanker, left port at Toledo in December 1942, escorted by the tugboat *Admiral*. However, the journey quickly took a turn for the worst. Traveling east, off the coast of Cleveland, something strange occurred. It was reported that the *Clevco* radioed around four a.m. that their escort, the *Admiral*, had mysteriously disappeared. The towline, which connected the two ships, was "at a low angle," as if the tugboat had sunk.

The *Clevco* quickly slowed to a halt and radioed the Coast Guard for help, who immediately sent two cutters and several motorboats to their location. Unfortunately, when the Coast Guard arrived, they found nothing. Both ships had vanished.

The Civil Air Patrol helped with searching for the *Clevco* and the *Admiral*. Eventually pilot Clara Livingston spotted the *Clevco* fifteen miles south; however, as soon as she reported the location to the Coast Guard, her radio went dead. She later reported a freak storm appeared, sending a cloud of snow upon the ship. The Coast Guard later arrived at the location, but found nothing.

Later, in the afternoon, a cutter named the *Ossipee* saw the *Clevco*, nearly close enough to board her. Yet, once again, another snow storm appeared and the ship vanished. Amazingly, hours later the *Clevco* was in radio contact with the Coast Guard, stating they were, "adrift and unable to steer." They communicated with the Coast Guard for over an hour, until the radio transmissions ceased, and the *Clevco* was never heard from again. Later, the next morning, bodies of two *Clevco* crew members were found, washed ashore near Cleveland.

The demise of the *Clevco* (and *Admiral* as well) is nothing new to the Great Lakes. The treacherous and unforgiving waterways are no stranger to tragedy ever since they were first explored back in the 1600s. At a moment's notice, monstrous storms can appear, easily taking ships and their crew to a watery grave.

But is the tragic demise of so many vessels due to natural forces? Or are they stemming from something supernatural? Many speculate, including author Jay Gourley and his 1977 book, *The Great Lakes Triangle*: the conclusion to such devastation many times lead to one primary force—The Storm Hag.

Legend has it the Storm Hag lives near Presque Isle Peninsula. The demonic wench has yellow eyes like a cat, with pale, green skin. Her teeth are pointy and sharp—like a shark, used to rip the skin off the crew she captures. Her teeth are green as well, giving her the legendary nickname—Jenny Greenteeth. Her fingers have pointy nails that are poisonous, able to paralyze anyone she confronts.

The legend also seems very similar to the classic "siren" story, where she sings a luring song to capture her prey. It's been said her favorite song to sing is the one from this chapter. Once you've heard her song, it's too late. A violent storm will soon appear, swallowing your ship and all the crew members. Or sometimes the storm will break, revealing a serene calm, just before she attacks. And to this day many who sail near Presque Isle can hear the phantom screams of the dead crews from long ago.

There's also the shadowy disappearance of Captain George Donner.

The Freighter *O.M. McFarland* left Presque Isle in April of 1937, setting sail for Port Washington, Wisconsin. After a long day he retired to his cabin for the night. He was not disturbed until the morning, when a shipmate went to his cabin, but he was nowhere to be found. It was as if he simply vanished—perhaps taken in the dead of night by the Storm Hag.

Whether you believe in the stories of the Storm Hag or not, with so many ships and crews disappearing to the depths of the Great Lakes, or that the vessels reach their early demise due to natural causes, it's clear the Great Lakes can be a very dangerous place to navigate. Regardless, you may want to think twice about taking a Great Lakes cruise if your captain has a nickname of Storm Hag, or if she's green-skinned with sharp, pointy teeth.

CHAPTER 10

The Red Devil of Detroit

A medieval painting depicting the evil creature known as the Red Devil, also known as the Nain Rouge, which most recently haunts the city of Detroit along Lake Michigan.

Angels and demons, that which stems from beyond, catering to our fears and horrific beliefs, are all too real for me. While I'm not entirely sure about angels, I do know that devils—in particular the likes of the Red Devil of Detroit—do in fact exist.

My name is Timothy Matthews, a young, handsome (so my wife tells me) family man. At one point, the White House claimed I would be the next up-and-coming politician. I worked my way up through the ranks, eventually running a swift and successful campaign for U.S. Congress, representing the great state of Michigan. Yet something went horribly wrong, all due to that cursed Red Devil—the Nain Rouge.

It was only weeks into my campaign, yet I could sense the momentum swinging in my direction. The competition was next to nothing, even though I battled a longtime incumbent congressman, rooted deeply in the trenches of government with his fourth term on the horizon. It seemed the town of Detroit, along with the rest of Michigan, readied themselves for change. Everyone, except for the Red Devil, that is.

My downfall began at that fateful party, sponsored by a local N.R.A. group. No, it had nothing to do with guns and someone going postal. Most of the engagement went smoothly, with lots of informal speeches and informal toasting. It wasn't until the end that I noticed the odd Goth women, slamming numerous glasses of champagne like water on a hot summer day.

She stood out from everyone else's tuxedos and formal gowns; she wore a short black leather skirt (showing off a multitude of slithering tattoos that wound down her slender legs), a black tee-shirt with the words "Freedom Sux" across her chest, and a matching leather jacket which seemed several sizes too small. Her hair had to be a wig, sprouting plastic red fluorescent strands, spiked in every direction. Her complexion was white, almost ghostlike, except for the purple lipstick and matching eyeliner. Oh, and did I mention the black cat gliding in and around her legs?

The last thing I should have done was to visit with her. There would be pictures taken, and I'd be on the front cover of all nationally inquisitive magazines, wondering why we were together. Yet I had no choice—something compelled me to see her, for better or for worse. Little did I know how "worse" it would be.

"Got a light?" she said as she pulled out a neatly rolled cigarette, no filter, smiling slightly.

I smiled back. "You know there's no smoking."

She patted the end of the cigarette on the lapel of my tux, smiling deeper now. "Yeah, but who cares."

I laughed, intrigued by her...probably in her twenties? She seemed to have the ambience and demeanor of someone decades older. I nodded, and then asked,

"So are you my number one fan?"

"Hardly," she quickly replied while twirling the unlit cigarette in her fingers. She reached down and gently pet the cat, then stood up briskly and leaned closer to me. "But I'm here to help." Then she reached up and yanked on my bow tie, bringing me uncomfortably close. She whispered, "I'm here to save you."

I pushed her gently back, trying to control my composure in front of the crowd, which by now had filtered in on me with shifting eyes. "Excuse me?" I said somewhat harshly.

She licked the cigarette, then popped it in her mouth and flung her head back, nearly sending her brilliant red wig to the floor. She turned back to me, her joking and relaxed expression void. With blinking, seriously green eyes, she said, "It's more of a warning."

My smile dropped, replaced by a chiseled and puckered face. "Get out."

Before I could react, she grabbed my hand, her palm against mine, and an explosion of painful visions began to dance through my head.

At first I was too numb to comprehend what had happened. It felt like an electrical storm had been unleashed into my head. Explosions and crackling emanated across my landscape, sending my senses into overdrive. When things finally cleared, I found myself viewing a man strapped tightly in a straightjacket, surrounded by white padded walls. The man looked terrified, frantic at the world around him, always looking over his shoulder and screaming at nothing. I felt pity on this man, until I realized who it was—it was me.

Several more visions appeared, all horrific and littered with terror that I would try hard to forget for the rest of my life. Yet before I knew it, the dread subsided, sending me reeling back into the reality of the night.

With sweat dripping from my forehead, I turned around the room, searching for the young Goth lady, but could find her nowhere. I asked several at the party, yet no one acknowledged her existence. Furthermore, they worried about my onslaught of craziness, bantering to some imaginary person in the room. I wondered if perhaps this was what happened when one lost his mind. Still, the only proof (for me at least) that I hadn't become totally senseless, was the black cat, which slowly sauntered between the legs of all those in the room, all the while looking at me with a slender smile and beady red eyes.

That night, while in bed, still shaken from the visions, I told my wife about the experience, trying desperately to laugh it off. She tried too, explaining it as a bad truffle, foul liver pâté, or pungent glass of champagne.

"You're right," I said while reaching over to stroke her back as she faced away from me.

"Of course, I'm right," she said, turning toward me. I leaned closer for a kiss; however, the face that greeted me was nothing like I'd ever seen before. Her skin had been replaced by a matted crimson red fur, her nose had become pushed inward and blackened like that of a cat, her teeth were like tiny, razor sharp daggers colored in different shades of brown. But it was the eyes that I feared most: beady red, glowing like tiny pools of phosphorous blood.

I pushed back fiercely from the creature that was once my wife, who now puckered profusely with its blackened crusty lips and yelled, "Kiss me!"

I screamed and began punching the creature, not believing this was happening. Yet there it was, in all its wretchedness, a sour-smelling beast covered in thick, matted, red hair. Anger filled my heart—how could this thing take my wife? Where was she? Did it *eat* her? I continued my assault, fueled by hatred, but my beating did little to thwart the little creature's advance.

The creature cackled loudly, all the while reaching at me, scratching and clawing. It couldn't have been any taller than four feet, and maybe weighed ninety pounds, yet its power was immense.

"What's the matter, Timothy? Don't you like me?" It cackled again, then opened its mouth wider than I thought possible, sending a streaming of plump juicy maggots in my direction and across the bed.

I swatted and scraped away the worms, only to find the creature had disappeared, replaced by my wife once again, who now was shrieking in terror with face bloodied beyond recognition. "Timothy!" she screamed, pulling herself out of bed. I screamed in horror, seeing what I had done to my wife. Yet it hadn't been my wife, that much I was sure of.

I had dialed for an ambulance, which showed up much later than needed. The police arrived sooner, and were very interested in my story. They didn't believe me of course—it was much too fantastical for anyone to believe. So I spent the night in jail for the first time ever. While my wife chose not to press charges, the damage had already been done. Over the next several days, I spent less time complaining about my experience with the Nain Rouge and more time defending what had happened. Nobody believed me. As the rumor mill spun away, my numbers in the polls plummeted. I began to question whether the Nain Rouge did in fact appear as my wife. Were the legends of Detroit's Red Devil true? Or perhaps I was simply going mad? Only time would tell.

Thankfully, the next few weeks went by without any sign of the Nain Rouge. Of course, my plans for being a politician were all but ruined. The only thing that saved me was that the other running candidate had his own dark past. Leaks of tax evasion, a secret mistress, and phone recordings of racial slurs surfaced, making it difficult for the guy to get anywhere. So with only a week before the election, I had managed to pull a full ten points ahead of him.

My only concern had to do with the Red Devil—would he appear to me again? While my belief in the creature dwindled, having chalked up my bad behavior in bed to be more of a temporary mental imbalance, I figured it couldn't hurt to do some research on the beastly legend—just in case, I suppose.

It turns out the Red Devil of Detroit has been seen by numerous people over the past century, and never with glad tidings. Bad things always happened to those he visited, which now may have included me. I just hoped my run in with the red furry dwarf had completed its course. Although I wished even more that I'd imagined the entire event.

As luck would have it, the Nain Rouge appeared again. It was the last day before elections, and proved also to be the last day of my known normal life. A press conference had been scheduled with the mayor to address the recent urban uprising. Those living within the slums of the inner city were revolting, sending Molotov cocktails through storefront windows, drive-by shootings in the wealthier neighborhoods, and countless buildings falling prey to the hands of arsonists.

The mayor read a prepared statement, covering the last few days of the urban assault on Chicago. He then did his best to quell the media frenzy unfolding, answering questions like any seasoned politician. Because we had been good friends since college, he invited me to the press conference, allowing me an opportunity to speak about the rioting and hopefully bumping my points in the poll to a safe and secure level.

The mob of reporters all began asking questions of me, but I pointed to the journalist preselected by the mayor, answering his pre-planned questions smoothly. I selected questions from the next appointed journalist, answering his questions prim and proper. But then a slew of unrehearsed questions came from the back. They were too loud to ignore, as if the journalist spoke through a megaphone. I tried to remain calm, smiling and smooth talking as best I could, but then I saw who was asking the questions—it was the Nain Rouge.

"You!" I screamed, ready to jump off the stage and attack the tiny red dwarf.

"Excuse me?" replied the Nain Rouge, looking confused.

"Him!" I yelled, pointing at the little red devil. "He's the one that hurt my wife!"

Everyone around the Nain Rouge looked perplexed. Something told me I was the only one seeing the creature in its true form. The Nain Rouge cleared its throat and asked, "So Timothy, is it true you believe in the Red Devil of Detroit?" The beast laughed and added, "Surely you can't accept such legends as truth." His lips curled outward, teeth clenched, sending a sadistic smile my way.

I stood my ground, responding with a controlled smile. "Of course not. There's

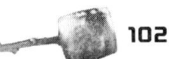

no such thing as the Red Devil." I looked the beast in the eyes and asked, "And what was your name again?"

The Red Devil, now beaming with satisfaction replied, "You can call me Mr. Red." He then pushed his way through the crowd, the reporters magically parting like Moses and the Red Sea. The Nain Rouge stood firmly in front of me and asked one more question. "So, Timothy, what's it like to be a wife beater?"

That's when I lost it. Looking back on the event, I should have had no problem controlling myself. I believe my emotions went into overdrive, fueled by the evil power surrounding the Nain Rouge. All I remember is leaping at the beast, dropping him to the ground and pounding and tearing through him. As the police pulled me off him and placed handcuffs on me, I looked back at the Red Devil, who had disappeared—replaced by a bloodied reporter with an obviously twisted neck.

Excerpts from the notes of the resident psychologist at St. Bernards Hospital, psychiatric ward

...Patient Timothy Matthews' initial assessment is serious at best. He is uncooperative and extremely hostile, resorting typically to being strapped to his bed. Will monitor progress to determine psychosis and potential treatment options...

...Patient Timothy Matthews's condition has become severe. Treatment with drugs and therapy have been inconclusive. He continues to speak about seeing a little, red, furry dwarf, known in legends as the Red Devil of Detroit, or the Nain Rouge. Mr. Matthews spends most of his time in solitary confinement, eats little food, and is virtually impossible to communicate with...

...Patient Timothy Matthews—final entry. Patient has taken his own life, hung by a strap from his straight jacket. It seems impossible for him to undo a single strap, let alone hang himself. Furthermore, reviewing surveillance tapes show something unusual at the time of his death. While the video quality is poor, a reddish blur can be seen flickering in and out of his cell, as if something is in there with him. Investigation is pending, but foul play is not being ruled out—although I'm not sure how anyone could have gotten into the locked cell, not to mention who would have the motive...

History

For anyone from Detroit, or other parts in and around Michigan, the Red Devil of Detroit is most likely no stranger. Also known as the Nain Rouge, legend has it that when the creature appears, something terrible is to come.

There are many variations of the story, depending on the book, author, or timing of publication. One of the oldest versions of the Nain Rouge came from the book, *Legends of Le Detroit*, published in 1883. The story back then went as such:

It was the year 1701, in Quebec (now known as St. Louis), and a gathering of celebration was in place to honor Antoine de la Mothe Cadillac, who would soon become the founder of Detroit. At one point during the story, a fortune teller with palm reading skills appeared with a large black cat perched on her shoulder. Many palms were read, amazing those around her, and eventually she came upon Antoine Cadillac.

The fortune teller impressed Mr. Cadillac with her ability to tell the future. Most importantly, she told him about founding a great city. Cadillac was excited, and pressed her for more information. But the fortune teller turned grim and responded, "In years to come, your colony will be the scene of strife and bloodshed. Indians will be treacherous, the hated English will struggle for possession, but under a new flag it will reach a height of prosperity, which you never in your wildest dreams could picture."

Cadillac's expression saddened, yet the fortune teller continued. "… beware of undue ambition; it will mar all your plans. Appease the Nain Rouge. Beware of offending him. Should you be thus unfortunate not a vestige of your inheritance will be given to your heirs."

Cadillac scoffed at her announcement of his bleak and unfortunate future, thinking her as just another carnival act. Yet years later, the fortune teller's words seemed to take shape. While walking with his wife, they heard two men complaining about their city, Detroit. "Things cannot run very long thus. My wife saw, a few days ago, le petit home Rouge." Cadillac's wife immediately became startled, as she knew 'le petit home Rouge' was in fact the Nain Rouge that the fortune teller had mentioned years before.

Cadillac ignored his wife's comment, up until an ugly-looking, dwarf-like creature crossed their path. It smiled at them with a sharp-toothed grin. Cadillac, annoyed with the creature stepping in front of them, struck it with his cane, telling it to go away. The red-colored dwarf laughed at Cadillac before it turned and hobbled away.

After that confrontation, Cadillac's life turned sour, and everything the fortune teller told him about his doomed future started to become true. His luck went dry, his children inherited nothing of his once-great fortune, fortifying the legend of the Nain Rouge, that the Red Devil of Detroit is a harbinger of doom.

Other Red Devil of Detroit sightings include:

- On July 30th of 1763, a red dwarf appeared near the Detroit River. That very next day, the Battle of Bloody Run occurred, with Chief Pontiac of the Ottawa tribe killing over sixty British soldiers.

- In 1805, the Nain Rouge was spotted wandering through the streets of Detroit. Then, shortly afterward, a horrific fire swept through town, burning most everything in its path.

- In 1813 General William Hull, the only officer in history to be sentenced to death for military incompetence, claims to have seen the Red Devil of Detroit "grinning at him" when he surrendered Detroit to the British army.

- It's been reported that the Nain Rouge has been spotted during the long riots of 1967.

- On March 1st, 1976, two utility workers spotted the Nain Rouge climbing a utility pole. Soon after that, one of the worst ice storms Detroit had ever experienced hit. That was the last-known reported sighting of the Red Devil in Detroit.

As you can see, the Nain Rouge is no stranger to Detroit—which means you may want to keep an eye out for any small, devil-like creatures wandering around late at night. And if you do see him, avoid all eye contact, and hope that he does not see you, or else bad luck will soon result.

CHAPTER 11

Niagara Falls' Maiden of the Mist

An eerie picture, perhaps representing the Maiden of the Mist, which has been reported to haunt Niagara Falls along the shores between Lake Erie and Lake Ontario.

The following are excerpts of the August 10th footage retrieved from the digital video card captured by Billy Windham and Charlie Ross at the base of Niagara Falls. Aside from a few bits of rubber raft, and an empty Styrofoam cooler, the video (though badly damaged) is all that remains of them.

August 10, 3:37 p.m.

Video begins with Billy and Charlie driving down Interstate 190, on their way to Niagara Falls. Billy is panning from windshield view to Charlie in the driver's seat.

"Here we go, baby!" yells Billy. "On the hunt!"

Charlie smiles and sips on a Genesee beer, then realizes the camera is running. His grin drops as he reaches over and slaps at Billy. "Hey man, you can't video me drinking beer! It's illegal."

Billy laughs, "Illegal because we're only eighteen, or because we're slamming them in a car!"

Charlie's smile returns and says, "Touché my ghost aficionado!" He gulps, finishing his beer, then loudly belches.

"What better way to end the summer!" says Billy, before letting out an equally loud burp in response to Charlie's. "Catching some ghosts, then on to be a college man!"

"Dude," says Charlie as he reaches in the backseat for another beer from the cooler, "not just any ghost—Maiden of the Mist!"

"Yeah, if we catch this beast on tape, we'll be the next Jason and Grant!"

"For sure," replied Charlie as he cracked open his brew. "With enough cameras, recorders, and a little luck, we'll get something. For sure."

August 10, 7:23 p.m.

Video filmed by Charlie, showing Billy setting up camp along the banks of Niagara River, with the evening sun dipping below the horizon.

Billy, struggling with the tent poles, frowns and turns to face the camera. "Are you gonna help me with this, or just sit their filming like you were Spielberg?"

"I'm more partial to Coppola, or maybe Tarantino."

"Whatever," says Billy, now throwing the tent poles into the darkness beyond.

Charlie laughs, "I think we'll be needing those." Charlie sets the camera on a nearby rock, continuing to record Billy's troubles. "This'll be a good YouTube video, on how *not* to setup a tent."

"Whatever," repeated Billy as he searches for the tossed tent poles. "Get over here and help me with this wild thing."

"It's just a tent," says Charlie as he begins to feed the found poles through the side of the tent.

"Okay, Mr. Boy Scout, show this city kid how it's done." Billy tosses the remaining poles at Charlie.

"It's not rocket science," responds Charlie as he points to the other end of the tent. "Hold it right there. That's good." He quickly slides the other pole through the opposite side, instantly springing the tent up into a usable form. "Mucho better compadre."

Billy smiles and says, "I think that's something we can sleep in."

"Probably no time for sleeping," replies Charlie as he fastens a stake into the tent corner. "We'll be hunting for our misty maiden most of the night."

"Maybe we'll get lucky and she'll come right to us. We snap a few pictures, shake her hand, then get a decent seven hours of sleep."

"Yeah, right," replies Charlie. "And maybe we'll win the lottery tonight, too."

"But we didn't buy any tickets."

"Exactly," replies Charlie, then both of them burst out laughing.

August 10, 9:12 p.m.

Video of crackling campfire, small but efficient in keeping them warm, and fending off the ghosts of the night.

"Watch it with the firewood," says Billy as he sips on a beer in his camp chair. "We don't want Smokey the Bear showing up."

"Good point," replies Charlie as he stabs at the burning embers, sending the fire flickering just above knee high. "But I figured it's a good deterrent from the Maiden of the Mist."

"You don't actually believe in it? I mean, it seems a little farfetched." Billy slams the remaining beer in his can. "I just came out here to party."

"Partying's good," replies Charlie, "but hunting ghosts is better." Charlie wrestles with the burning logs, stirring up a taller fire. "Don't tell me you're a skeptic, or did you lie about your ghostly encounter? And what about all those EVPs we collected at old man Winter's place?"

"Yeah, I know. There's something real about them. Just not sure about this Maiden of the Mist."

"There's only one way to find out," says Charlie as he reaches for another beer from the cooler. At the same time he looks out over the water at something twinkling. "Say, what's out there?"

Billy peers beyond the shoreline for a moment, his face filled with excitement. His expression turns sour as he says, "Crap, I think it's a boat—and it's heading toward us!"

Charlie begins kicking at the fire, trying to put it out. Billy reaches forward, frantically dumping beer on it as well. The fire eventually goes out, with Billy and Charlie running into the darkness, beyond the illumination of the night vision IR

camera. A light from the river approaches, with the sputter of a small boat engine lingering. The video continues for the next few minutes, with a boat clearly marked D.N.R on the side, sweeping the shores with a light, in obvious pursuit of the once-glowing campfire. The boat eventually moves away, further down the dark, splashing river, leaving behind nothing but the sounds of waves gently slapping against the shoreline.

Billy and Charlie are eventually seen sneaking back to the dark coals of the campfire. Billy laughs and says, "Man, that was close."

"Yeah, the last thing I wanted to do was spend the weekend in jail, not to mention trying to explain to authorities about our crazy adventure."

"It's not so strange," replies Billy. "Nothing wrong with doing a little shoreline camping. Oh, and hunting for a haunting."

"Let's get that fire going again, then think through what we're going to do out there on the river. Probably a good idea, what with Niagara Falls looming in the distance."

Billy laughs and says, "Yeah, and I forgot my barrel. So no rides over the falls tonight."

"What, my inflatable raft' isn't good enough for you? By the way, someone should start blowing it up."

"Someone, as in me?" asks Billy.

"We can take turns. With the foot pump it shouldn't take too long."

The video continues, with the two young men once again setting up the campfire, taking turns inflating the raft, and then settling down into their camp chairs. They huddle over a map illuminated by the soft glow of their headlamps. Suddenly, a huge splashing sound can be heard from the dark, rippling shoreline nearby.

"What was that?" exclaims Charlie while standing up and turning toward the river.

"I dunno," replies Billy. "Something big though." Another splash is heard, this time louder and closer, with the resulting waves crashing to shore.

"Holy crap," whispers Charlie, "I think it's coming toward us."

Before either one of them can react, a large, elongated beast erupts from the tranquil shoreline, slithering its way through the sand.

"Oh my god! What is that!" screams Billy.

"Get the camera!" yells Charlie.

"Are you nuts? I'm not going anywhere near that thing!"

Charlie can be seen staring at Billy in disgust, shaking his head. "Wimp," was all that Charlie said as he ran breakneck speed toward the camera, keeping well away from the beastly snake creature. Thankfully, the tent was in the monster's path, slowing the thing down slightly. The giant snake hit the tent, rumbling through the nylon structure, as if it wasn't there.

Charlie had just enough time to grab the camera and run. Video now becomes shaky, with sporadic footage of the tree canopy above, the sandy ground beneath them, and a snake-like creature bearing down from behind. Charlie can be heard yelling. "Come on! Head for the raft!"

August 10, 11:23 p.m.

Video of Billy on the raft, stabilizing himself against the rocking waves, and not looking at all too pleasant.

"Can we go back now?" asks Billy, who keeps peering out into the darkness of the river with his handheld night vision camera. "We've been out here for hours, and nothing has shown up."

"Relax," replies Charlie, "It's been less than two hours." The video becomes jumbled for a moment, then settles down revealing both young men. "There, that's better. Just hope the raft mount you made doesn't break and send our video to the bottom of the river."

"Duct tape to the rescue," says Billie with a smile, his mood finally lightening. "You know, I don't understand how you get me into these situations. Ghost hunting is one thing, in the safe confines of some creaky old house. But out on a river, less than a mile from the impending doom of the falls—this is just plain stupid."

"Stupid, maybe," replies Charlie. His face lights up with a beaming grin. "But isn't this just freaking amazing?"

Billie returns a cheery smile. "Yeah, I suppose. Beats sitting back home watching reruns of *Ghost Hunters*. Pass me another beer."

Charlie laughs. "Yeah, I can't believe you wouldn't rescue the camera, but you nearly got chomped in two by the beastly snake trying to save the beer cooler."

"A guy's gotta have his priorities," replies Billy as he cracks open another beer.

Minutes go by in silence, save for the splashing of gentle waves against the raft. The low rumble of Niagara Falls can be heard in the distance. Billy can be seen with his handheld night vision camera peering once again into the waters around them. Suddenly *(from Billy's camera),* the head of a large serpent appears, mouth wide open revealing several sets of sharp jagged teeth, then dives below.

"Holy crap!" yells Billie as his camera swivels around to face Charlie. "Did you see that?"

"See what?" asks Charlie as he adjusts the raft-mounted camera.

"It's here again! The snake monster thing!"

Charlie turns around calmly. "Relax. I'm sure it's no big deal—probably a giant carp."

"Carps are bottom dwellers," replies Billy. "And I don't think the river is that shallow."

"Let's see the video," says Charlie. The next few minutes are spent with Charlie reviewing Billy's video. "Oh my god!" yells Charlie. "That thing is huge!"

Both of them can be seen sliding to the center of the raft, all the while looking around in the water, no doubt concerned about their safety.

"Maybe we should head for shore," asks Billy.

"Yeah, probably a good idea."

The two young men cautiously paddle toward the nearest shoreline, but not before the great snake-beast strikes. The video shows the raft flying upward, with Billy and Charlie screaming, terrified. A glimpse of the creature can be seen, its glowing eyes and dagger teeth twinkling in the night-vision camera.

August 11, 12:42 a.m.

Video shows Charlie, panting heavily, hanging onto a buoy.

"Man, I can't believe we survived that," says Charlie, occasionally surveying the waters around them.

"Not over yet," says Billy, breathing deeply. "And we lost the boat." A slight pause, then he adds, "We gotta figure out how to get back to shore."

"Or wait for sunlight?" asks Charlie.

"What good would that do? You think the snake creature is afraid of sunlight, like it's some kind of vampire?"

"Might be," says Charlie, nodding his head hopefully.

"We don't have a choice," says Billie. "If we stay in this water much more than an hour, hypothermia will set in. We gotta make a run for it. Just need to make sure we don't get too close to the falls."

"You can run if you want to," says Charlie, forcing a smile, "but I'm gonna try swimming." He peers into the dark water around them, hesitant. While it appears to be calm, with gentle lapping waves off the buoy, Charlie does not look at ease. Then he forces a smile and says, "So much for the Maiden of the Mist. We have a new monster to report on. Who'd a thought there'd be a sea serpent lurking in the waters of Niagara."

"Lake serpent, to be exact," replies Billy. "Yeah, this beats any ghostly maiden by far. Just hope we live to tell about it."

"You and me both, kid." Charlie looks around the water again, his eyes widening as he motions to Billy. "Guess it's time. Come on, let's go."

Charlie pushes off from the buoy, paddling in the murky waters. Within seconds the serpent attacks. The struggle is swift, with little screaming from Charlie as the beast opens its jagged mouth, pulling him down into the depths and darkness of the river. The camera is jittery, with Billy screaming in the background as the tape ends.

August 11, 1:07 a.m.

Video shows Billy filming himself, obviously still terrified and traumatized by the loss of his friend, who is nowhere to be found.

"This video's for you, Charlie." Fear can be seen in Billy's eyes as he still clings desperately to the wavering buoy, the camera shaking badly—not just from the violence that just unfolded, but no doubt from the beginning phases of hypothermia. "We're gonna film this to the end." Slight pause as Billy turns the camera to look out into the dark waters beyond.

The camera returns to Billy's face. "Whoever gets this video, let the world know there's something out here—something deadly. It's got nothing to do with that stupid story about the Maiden of the Mist. It's everything about—" The camera turns to the water again, this time something is visible, bobbing just out of reach. Billy screams, realizing it is the remains of Charlie.

The serpent strikes again, pulling Charlie down for good. The video becomes choppy, as it seems Billy tries desperately to climb on top of the buoy, but to no avail.

Silence settles in for several minutes as Billy tries to film the water around him, obviously panicked beyond belief. Eventually he sees signs of movement, with the all too familiar serpent head slithering in the water—heading toward Billy for its next meal.

Then, somewhere off camera, a brilliant white light shines. Billy pans the camera toward it, revealing a silhouette of some glowing figure, descending to him. The giant snake, seemingly just as perplexed as Billy, stops its pursuit momentarily, and then begins shrieking wildly.

The glimmering figure has now floated to just above the waterline, and can clearly be seen as a woman in white—the Maiden of the Mist no doubt.

Billy moves the camera toward the giant serpent, who in a last-ditch effort is lunging toward Billy. The Maiden of the Mist can be heard off camera softly commanding, "No. This one is not for you." Billy pans out to capture the Maiden in Mist with her arm extended toward the beast. "This one is not for you," she repeats.

Like a frightened puppy, the snake arches back, shrieking one last time before diving below the surface.

Billy turns his camera to the glowing Maiden of the Mist. She has a serene smile and gazes mildly at Billy. "You… saved me," says Billy. "Thank you."

The Maiden of the Mist, not necessarily acknowledging Billy's appreciation, simply commands in her soft but firm voice, "Come with me."

"Billy briefly turns the camera on himself, showing a shivering but beaming smile. "Charlie, this one's for you. We did it! We got the Maiden of the Mist!"

"Come with me," she repeats, holding her hand out for Billy to receive as she floats delicately above the water.

"With pleasure," replies Billy, obviously mesmerized by her long flowing golden brown hair and tall slender body, a beauty beyond perfection.

As Billy touches her hand, he begins to rise from the water, floating alongside her. "Whoa," he says, amazed at the experience. "I feel light as a feather."

Billy pans up to the Maiden of the Mist, revealing her breathtaking smile and beauty as they float across the water. Moments later, Billy pans farther away, in the direction they are traveling. He can clearly hear the rumble of Niagara Falls getting louder, and see the mist getting thicker. The camera begins to become jittering, no doubt from the fear mounting in Billy. "That's not the way to shore." A struggle ensues as Billy tries to free his hand from the Maiden of the Mist. "Stop!" he yells as he looks up to her face—which is not the former beauty it once was. Instead, a hideous and ghoulish expression appears, with sunken eyes, rotting flesh, and sharp, dagger-like teeth from a demonic mouth opened wide.

Billy screams, trying desperately to break from the Maiden of the Mist's grip. With Niagara Falls just a few feet away, and mist rising before them thick as pea soup, the Maiden of the Mist can be heard commanding, "You are mine."

History

While the prior story is most intriguing, with the proposed video footage capturing the horrific events, sadly there is no record of any such case. Yet where did this myth come from?

This tale stems from the legendary Lady in the Mist, closely hovering around Niagara Falls between Lake Erie and Lake Ontario. There are many versions; the story is so popular that many boat tours around the falls are called "Maiden of the Mist." One thing is for sure, the legend does exist—but what is the truth surrounding the myth?

One of the original legends comes to us centuries ago, passed down through the generations of the Ongiaras Native American tribe. A young, beautiful woman lost her husband early on in their marriage and could not get over her sorrow. One day she climbed into her canoe, singing the songs of the siren—a death song—and paddled out into the swift current of the mighty Niagara River.

The canoe began to pitch and turn as it struggled against the churning waves, as she approached the falls. At the last moment she willingly left the canoe, heading over the edge of the falls. Yet Heno, the god of thunder who lived underneath the falls, felt pity for her and caught the maiden gently in his arms. He brought her peacefully to his home, behind the crashing curtain of falling water.

The grieving maiden was tended to by Heno and his sons, until her heart felt better. But not before Heno's younger son grew fond of the maiden, and soon they were married. The two of them spawned a young son, who followed Heno everywhere to understand what it was like being the god of thunder.

Eventually, the maiden and mother of the young son grew anxious to see her tribe again. She longed to see them, and soon got her wish—but not in a positive way. A giant snake had slithered through the Niagara River and turned the water toxic, poisoning her tribe. The terrifying snake planned to kill and devour them all. The maiden pleaded with Heno for help, to save her tribe. Heno brought the maiden to her people so she could warn them of the snake. The tribe then moved to higher ground, away from the water and snake, thus saving them.

At this point in the story, the legend seems to vary. In some cases, the giant snake is caught and killed by Heno, yet the remains of the humongous snake float down river and destroy his home, making him fly into the sky where he lives today (which makes sense if you are the god of thunder).

Other versions indicate that after the great sickness from the poisoned water, the tribe would send beautiful young maidens over the falls every year, to appease the thunder god Heno (also known as Hinum). But sometimes that was not enough. Eventually, the Chief of the tribe had to offer his own daughter in an effort to please the sons of the thunder god. The Chief's daughter, Lelawalo, was incredibly beautiful, making the decision for the chief difficult.

As Lelawalo plummeted to her death in Niagara Falls, the sons of Heno saved her. She agreed to stay with the sons, provided she could warn her village of the giant snake.

Just as Lelawalo began her plunge to certain death over the mighty cataracts of Niagara Falls, Heno's sons rescued her in their arms. They took her back behind the Falls and, mesmerized by her beauty, they implored her to stay with them. Understanding that her main destiny was to save her village, she agreed on one condition. She asked to know what was killing the people of her village. Heno's sons agreed to tell her and allow her to return to share the answer to the mystery with the village. And it's said that the Maiden of the Mist can still be seen over the falls, protecting everyone who approaches.

There are several other versions, but all seem to carry a similar trait; there's a Maiden of the Mist near Niagara Falls, protecting people from harm. Then again, according to the tale in the beginning of this chapter, she may be the last thing you ever see.

So the next time you visit Niagara Falls, enjoying one of the many boat tours available, think about the Maiden of the Mist, but don't be too eager for her rescue—she may be hungry for your soul and you hear the words lightly whispered, "You are mine."

A mysterious picture of a ghostly girl, possibly like the White Lady haunting the shores of Lake Ontario near Rochester, New York.

CHAPTER 12

The White Lady of Lake Ontario

You never know what you're getting into when you purchase an old house. There's the usual suspects, such as a rattling furnace, rusty water pipes, and even the occasional loose shingle. What I didn't expect was being haunted—no terrorized— by the Lady in White.

The small, single-story rambler fit my bachelor needs perfectly. No need to for anything too large—that just meant more to clean. And that's something I had no desire to do. My hopes were high in finding a girl who either loved to clean, or loved to live messy. Only time would tell. And being in New York, there were plenty of girls to choose from. But that did not, in my opinion, include the ghoulish Lady in White.

The location of the house intrigued me the most—just a stone's throw from Lake Ontario, right off nearby Durand Eastman Park. The price was right too, having been for sale well over a year, most likely due to the fallout in the housing market, or so I thought. I had no complaints, at least not until the second night after I moved in.

To keep me company, I offered to dog sit my parent's Yorkshire terrier, Maxwell, who had a bark that would make Godzilla proud, at least that's what Max thought. Unfortunately, he stood not more than shin high. Max didn't seem to care about something as insignificant as size; no dog was too large for him. Ghosts, on the other hand, were an entirely different matter.

Max and I had completed our move in, resting comfortably numb, while devouring food from a local Chinese takeout restaurant along with a glass of delicious plum wine. Okay, Max had none of this, but chewed happily on a new bone—twice his size mind you. I figured we were due for a celebration.

Thankfully, the cable had been setup, allowing us the pleasure of watching some TV. With the sun set, the lights dimmed, Max and I ate heartily in front of the boob tube with our favorite Travel Channel show playing—*Bizarre Foods*. I'll admit the reception could have been better, with a sporadic fuzziness making it difficult to determine what the host Andrew popped into his mouth. Then again, it didn't matter. Chances are it was something bizarre, although not as bizarre as what happened next.

I was just polishing off my large helping of Kung Pao chicken, when the TV signal began to get fuzzy. Real fuzzy. Eventually, nothing remained except the white noise background and matching sound.

"Come on!" I yelled, slamming my fist with chopsticks onto my plate, sending small bits of spicy chicken and fried rice into the confines of my recliner. I turned to Max, who immediately began eyeing up the sprayed Chinese food. I said, "Not good, Max. Not good." Then I waved my chopsticks at Max, motioning toward the TV. "See if you can fix the dumb boob tube."

Max ignored me completely, focused intently on his mammoth chew bone, which he had hardly made a dent in. But then he stopped, turning toward the fuzzy TV picture, and growled.

"It's nothing, boy," I said reassuringly. I turned to look at the TV and quickly realized something strange indeed was happening.

The black and white fuzzy screen began to take shape, forming a face of some sort. A woman's perhaps? Long hair seemed to drape down each side within the noisy peppered frame. A head floated in and out of the white crackling haze, making me pull forward for a closer look. Then, at the last second, the picture reached clarity, revealing a woman ghostly white staring back. She had a depressingly sad face, with her pupils like blackened pools of tar, her lips just as dark. Max began to bark wildly. The gloomy expression on the young woman then took a turn for the worse as her jaw opened inhumanly wide, and her eyes flared to a deep, crimson red. An intense scream erupted from the screen, forcing me to cover my ears and for Max to turn tail and run for the safety of the bedroom.

In an instant, the ghostly apparition had vanished, leaving me to wonder if it actually happened. Andrew from *Bizarre Foods* came back on the TV, appearing in full form and discussing the culinary options when cooking sheep testicles. I looked at the almost empty plate of Kung Pao, then over to my glass of plum wine, then over to where Max had scampered to. "Max! Maxwell!" I looked at the TV and added quietly to myself, "Nothing to be scared of."

The next supernatural event occurred a few weeks later. Max continued to stay with me on the weekends, and we had settled into an exercise routine late at night, namely jogging. I had never been the most athletic person; my belief in running only occurred when you were being chased by something bigger than yourself. Still, Max needed his exercise, and it certainly couldn't hurt me, right? Little did I know…

At first we tried late afternoon walks instead of jogging, but I quickly found out Max had the mind of a greyhound. I wondered if he might be worthy of a marathon or two, or some doggy sprinting across town. Even with his miniscule legs, he could really move, putting many of my two-legged friends to shame—including myself. So the walking became jogging, and with my usual lack of time management, the sun typically set by the time we marched out into the street.

I got used to the jogging routine. It helped living next door to Durand Eastman Park. There were lots of great jogging paths, and lots of places for Max to explore. Our typical pattern brought us along a foundation of some sort, perhaps an old building or house. Most nights there were no issues; however, occasionally, Max would get spooked, which of course got the hair on my neck standing. The other night was the worst—even I could feel the spookiness, like it floated through the air nearby. Of course, that's exactly what was happening.

As we turned the corner and approached the old foundation, I instantly knew something was wrong. Max could feel it too and began growling at something just beyond the light of the street lamp. The warm, August evening turned chilly as a damp fog rolled in from the lake. I shivered as I watched my breath condense and curl up into the air. I instinctively tugged Max closer and said weakly, "Come on Max. It's nothing."

We continued our exercise, now more a cautious saunter than anything. "It's nothing," I repeated to Max, whose bark had become a whimper as he dove in and around my legs.

As the mist grew heavy, a figure appeared, hovering high above ground at first, then descending to the path in front of us. It appeared to be a woman, ghostly white, blending nicely with the fog, and now only a few feet from us. The apparition blocked our path; I thought at first about turning to run, but then scoffed at the idea. I didn't believe in ghosts. Furthermore, from what I knew, you didn't want to run away—you needed to stand your ground and let the fiendish ghoul know you were not afraid. The only trouble was in how freakishly scared I had become, nearly wetting my pants.

I chose to march forward, sluggishly at first, ignoring the ghostly apparition, tugging at the leash around Max, who had no intentions of moving. Apparently my advancement offended her, for she opened her coal black mouth and let out a scream that had to have echoed all the way to the Canadian shores across Lake Ontario. That's when I got a good look at her face. It was faded, pale white, with sunken eyes behind bony, white cheeks. And her eyes were blackened pools, seeming to be filled with death and despair. And the sadness—she reeked of it—I could feel it emanating, penetrating my mind and body. Depression weighed heavily on my heart, causing me to stumble. That's when she attacked.

It didn't feel physical, like being struck with a fist or baseball bat, or nothing that could permanently damage my body. The attack seemed to be more like a battle played out in my head. It felt like my soul had been tugged at, being stretched outward from my body. I struggled, lunging randomly at the air around me, trying desperately to grab the Lady in White before my lifeforce disappeared forever. Yet she, like my soul, was made of nothing physical. I would have ended up dead that night, with a lifeless body limp on the jogging path and devoid of any soul—but Max, my faithful steed, saved me.

Max began barking wildly, lashing out at the phantom creature as it busily tore through my soul. It seemed like Max could see the Lady in White, knowing exactly where to gnash and bite. Eventually, the ghoulish creature gave up, shrieking frantically and ascending into the mist from whence it came. Max and I had won that battle, but somehow I knew there would be more.

Weeks had gone by with no additional ghostly incidents. I began to feel confident that she would no longer bother me—Max had done his job well enough. Of course, just to be safe, we put our nightly weekend jogs on hold. Instead, we switched to bike riding, trying hard to peddle our way to healthiness prior to sunset. Unfortunately, my time management skills were not improving much, and we ended up biking in the light of the moon.

Obviously, I was the one biking—Max spent most of his time trying to keep up. While he was a maniac on the jogging course, he struggled with bicycles. But I wanted to ride a bike, thinking it would give me a better chance at escaping from the Lady in White, if we ever ran into her again—which in time did occur.

The sun had set as usual, leaving Durand Eastman Park sparsely populated with people. Max and I peddled through the trees along the ponds with our path illuminated by only the moon and streetlights. We felt confident in our expedition. After all, the ghostly Lady in White hadn't appeared for weeks. Maybe it was just a hallucination? But, just as we turned the corner and traveled by the old foundation, a thick, heavy mist appeared once again out of nowhere.

We had no time to react. She darted out of the fog with lightning speed and descended directly in front of us. She pushed her hands forward, then emanated an unearthly scream, sending Max and I backward, tumbling away from the bike.

Thankfully, I had released my grip on Max's leash before my crash, which sent him rolling only briefly to the soft grass in the ditch. Still, I did not see him climb out. I briefly checked my own body and found no serious injuries. I turned just in time to see the Lady in White screaming toward me, confident in her revenge and readying herself to steal my soul.

I, on the other hand, had something else planned. Call me crazy, but I brought a few supernatural items along with me, concealed in my backpack. I quickly zipped open the pack, revealing a bottle of Holy Water and a cross. I had done my research—just in case. Of course, I had no clue whether it would help my predicament, but it definitely sounded better than just screaming and whimpering like a little puppy. Heck, I even brought some garlic and a few wooden stakes—I didn't want to take any chances.

I quickly opened up the bottle of Holy Water, sprinkling randomly in the direction of the Lady in White. She stopped her attack, but only briefly. I'm not sure if it had anything to do with the Holy Water, but I didn't stand around to ask. Next I revealed my cross and yelled, "In the name of Jesus Christ, leave us be!" I said this several times, each time louder than before, and again this seemed to slow her down.

I'm convinced nothing I brought helped for long. In the end, it had been Max with the rescue. He made his way out of the ditch and on to the ankles of the phantom ghost, gnawing like they were solid bony treats. To this day, I don't know why but that Lady in White backed away from little old Maxwell—not so much from fear, but perhaps in respect?

With our jogging and biking adventures put on hold indefinitely, Max and I decided to try our hand at swimming. My parents thought I was crazy for taking a dog swimming, but they were adamant that he get exercise. So why not swimming? What's the worst that could happen?

As usual, I could not get out the door until it was dark. I have to admit, swimming under the pale moon light was quite exhilarating. Although I quickly realized swimming at night made it difficult to find Max with his dark brown hair; it was like spotting a lump of coal in a tar pit. Thankfully, there was enough moonlight for me to keep an eye on him. The sound of his splashing also helped, allowing me to easily hone in on his location.

I knew it was a bad idea to be swimming late at night, what with all the ghostly incidents that had occurred to us. But I didn't want a little thing like some crazy story about a Lady in White deter Max and me from enjoying life. Unfortunately, she had other ideas.

Just as Max and I finished our evening swim in Lake Ontario, and making us think we had cheated fate by not running into the Lady in White, she appeared out of nowhere. She floated in front of us as we swam to the shoreline. This time she didn't seem so threatening. In fact, I could almost detect a smile on her face. As we neared the shore, she motioned with her arm, beckoning us forward, all the while displaying a pale porcelain smile.

While I was quite relieved with her pleasant demeanor, Max didn't buy it. No sooner had he arrived on dry land, shaking off his thoroughly drenched coat, when he proceeded to bark profusely at the Lady in White. "Calm down," I said. "She doesn't seem so scary this time."

The Lady in White began to float backward, heading deeper into the tree canopy of Durand Eastman Park. I wondered for a moment if she might be afraid of the water? Perhaps she only wanted to lure us to dry land, and then snatch away our souls. Could a ghost be afraid of anything?

With Max barking in stubborn defiance, I hooked him to the leash and followed the ghostly lady into the forest. It probably wasn't the smartest thing I've ever done in my life. But she seemed so innocent and alluring. I had to go—it was like she had a spell on me. I trudged on, following her into the darkness, and into my most probable demise. And, for the first time, I realized the level of beauty she possessed—this lady was gorgeous and mesmerizing. I didn't care how dead she was, I need to be with her. She was a glowing fountain of pale white light that I could have easily followed off a cliff. Which was indeed her plan all along.

Before I knew it, we were walking along the steep embankment of the rocky shoreline not too far from my house. One false step and I would be ripped to shreds on the jagged rocks below. Max followed along, barking all the more at the phantom figure, trying desperately to nip at her translucent heals.

We continued on to an even more treacherous part of the rocky shoreline, my smile matching hers; I was transfixed on her illuminating beauty—beyond caring for my own life. I would do anything to be with her, and she knew it—jumping out and being impaled on the sharp rocks wasn't out of the question. Max, however, had other ideas.

Max gave up on his relentless pursuit of the Lady in White. Instead, he turned his attack on me. I felt a sharp pain on my left ankle, awakening me from my demonic trance. I looked down to see the little Terrier nipping at my heal.

"Max! Stop it!" That's when I looked at the Lady in White. Gone was her angelic and radiant smile, replaced by all things demonic. She screeched, revealing fangs that dripped something black and tar-like, oozing down her chin and smelling worse than a rotting carcass.

I started to back away, realizing my predicament. "Come on, Max. We should probably get out of —"

At that moment she let out an ear-splitting screech. I covered my ears and dropped to the ground, rolling partway onto the jagged rocks. Disoriented, I rolled around, my knees and feet stretching and pushing among the sharp boulders. I could tell my legs were getting cut badly, and knew I had to get out of there.

"Run, Max, Run!" I yelled, climbing away from the rocks and onto the soft grass.

The Lady in White maintained her loud screeching, both in amplitude and pitch, until I thought I would pass out. In a last gasp, I screamed back, "No!" And with that, her screaming subsided, along with her glowing personification. She had gone, leaving Max and myself with ringing ears and the gentle lapping waves against the Lake Erie shoreline.

"Come on," I said to Max as I stumbled to my feet. "Gotta get out of here."

We walked briskly back to my house, all the while looking behind for any signs of the Lady in White. Thankfully, she never appeared. We reached our house, went inside and immediately locked the door. I then went room to room, turning on all the lights. I looked down to Max, who by now was as pleasant as ever, sitting patiently by the pantry door, wagging his tail rapidly. I reached down to pet him and said, "Good boy, Max. Thanks for saving me again."

That's when the front door burst open, sending wooden splinters across the room, nearly impaling us.

Standing in the doorway was the Lady in White, her dress flowing in an unnatural swirling wind, illuminated by an even more unnatural glow from behind.

"Where is my baby!" she shrieked. I could hear barking—not from Max, but from something behind her on four legs. Phantom dogs perhaps? "My baby!" she repeated, now with outstretched arms.

This was not happening, I thought to myself. *This ghost stuff is just plain crazy.* Dream or not, I needed to either wake up from this nightmare, or deal with the demonic lady in front of me.

I mustered up my courage and waving my arms I yelled, "Get out of here!" I had no idea if that would do the trick. Actually, I thought it was probably the stupidest thing I've done, second only to swimming in the lake. Still, the statement seemed to startle the Lady in White, slowing her progress into the house.

"There's no baby here!" I yelled, going along with her concern. She stopped her pursuit, and then began a stare down that would be etched into my brain for the rest of my life. Her jet black eyes turned a dull gray, then to hazel. Her ghoulish grin disappeared, replaced by a smile of indifference. She no longer looked menacing, but more content and pleased. Then, within a few seconds, she faded away, leaving Max and me alone in the silence of the pale moonlight as it shimmered through the splintered front door.

History

The White Lady is a one of the more common ghostly spirits claimed to haunt people, from one end of the world to the other. The story here is no exception, in this case happening off the shores of Lake Ontario, near Irondequoit and Rochester, New York.

Legend has it that many of the white ladies stem from being victims of an injustice, typically due to an abusive lover or husband causing ill to them. The ghost will usually wear a white Victorian dress, and become an omen of death for anyone (typically men) crossing her path.

As for the White Lady of Ontario, the story begins in the early 1800s, where a woman, sometimes known as Eelissa, lived on the land with her dogs and daughter, currently part of Durand Eastman Park, near Rochester, New York. They lived comfortably in a cabin off the lake, until one day the daughter vanished. Concerned for her safety, the mother quickly searched the marshlands and shorelines. Days passed with no daughter to be found. Sorrow filled the mother's heart, as she feared the worst. She searched with the aid of her dogs, but still no luck. This went on for weeks. Eventually, with her heart heavy and filled with grief, she threw herself into Lake Ontario and died. Her dogs, now howling with sorrow, followed her into the lake and drowned.

Yet even death could not stop the mother's pursuit in finding her daughter's body. It is said that to this day, when the fog is thickest, you can sometimes see the White Lady rising from Durand Lake near Ontario, accompanied with her spectral dogs. They continuously search the park and surrounding areas for her missing daughter.

And if anyone is unfortunate enough to cross her path late at night around Durand Park, they will have a tale to tell no one will forget. Especially men: she looks for vengeance against males who she thinks murdered and raped her daughter. Many reports have been made of a White Lady in the mist chasing young men into the lake, or shaking their cars parked nearby, or hounding them until they leave the park.

Other reports have claimed to see her around the proposed foundation of her house. Many feel a powerful inner feeling of sadness as they stand nearby.

It's been reported that several males have experienced the wrath of the White Lady. A group of young men went to Durand Eastman Park late at night, around two a.m. They sat by the tree, which is known as the White Lady's Tree, down the hill next to Zoo Road. After a moment of silence, they began asking questions directed to the White Lady. Immediately one of the young men's phones began to beep, like random numbers were being pressed. Soon everyone's phone batteries drained. When they started asking about the killing of the White Lady's daughter, the tree began to glow in a bright white light. They quickly left the park and never returned.

Paranormal investigators have visited the park. Yet they are not drawn to the old foundation of the White Lady's house. Instead, they are pulled to an embankment on the east side, possibly the real location of the daughter's demise—maybe the case of a simple accidental drowning? Then again, it's claimed that no body has ever been found. As the investigators approached a nearby ravine, they seemed to hear a little girl screaming, "Mother! Mother! I'm down here Mother!" Later, the investigators heard on their audio recorders, "They pushed me down here, Mother!"

There are conflicting stories about the location of the White Lady's house, or White Lady's Castle, as some call it. Research shows the old foundation may in fact be what's left of a Lakeside Inn, demolished in the 1940s. Also, there is evidence of a murder in the area, but this occurred further inland.

The White Lady of Ontario has even reached the ranks of Hollywood movies. Filmmaker Frank LaLoggia directed a movie titled, *Lady in White* (1988) based on the story of the White Lady. Some of the movie was actually shot in the Rochester, New York, area.

Whether you believe the White Lady of Ontario tale is true or not, and with so many eyewitness accounts, it does appear as though something strange *is* happening. Perhaps this gives you an opportunity for a vacation to the area. Just be careful for you guys out there—I don't recommend jogging through the park late at night, unless you have a fearless Yorkshire terrier with you.

Monstrous fish, perhaps swimming near the shores of the Great Lakes, waiting for you to take a swim—if you dare.

Conclusion

It's easy to get wrapped up in a good ghost story, succumbing to its spookiness and perhaps scaring you into a sleepless, well-lit night. In the case of these Great Lakes tales, maybe you will never want to sail or swim in a lake again, or a bathtub for that matter. Seriously though, as I indicated in the beginning of this book, water tends to attract all things supernatural, with it acting as a conduit or catalyst for restless spirits. With the Great Lakes being such large bodies of water, it's no wonder there's a lot of supernatural things going on.

From Ghosts at Glensheen, to the Michigan Dogman, to the Red Devil of Detroit, it's clear there's a strangeness in the air, happening in and around all five of the Great Lakes. But is it because of the water or because of something else?

After all, there are stories of the supernatural around the world—nowhere near large bodies of water. What could be the connection to so many oddities occurring?

If the paranormal activity was due to the water, one might think there would be hundreds and thousands of documented incidents around the lakes. Then again, perhaps there are. There may be countless events, but most go either unnoticed or not recorded. Regardless, one thing for sure is that there are indeed many reports around the Great Lakes of supernatural occurrences. Of course, the best way to find out is for you to visit them yourself.

I've personally made it to Lake Superior and Lake Michigan, and have been truly amazed at their sheer size. It's like sailing on the ocean, where in some cases you easily lose sight of land. So as far as monsters of the deep go, I could certainly see that as a plausible situation, what with ample space to live and an abundant food source.

Yet why don't we have more reportings of them? How come they are so elusive? Some say they have evolved over millions of years to become super-intelligent beings, able to teleport in and out of time and space. In my opinion, I could think of better places to live in the universe than at the bottom of a lake.

The same could be true for the ghostly hauntings. Why do the ghosts stay put, whether it is in their mansion, or a park where their cabin once stood? With the spirit free from the body, I would hope they could travel faraway to other amazing places. I imagine there's no option for them—either they are condemned to a specific location until they are ready to move on, or maybe they love their place so much they never want to leave.

Someday soon, we may have the answer to why ghosts exist and why they do what they do. All it takes is for technology to continue to become more sophisticated. It may allow us to better analyze more and more data at a nano-scopic level—perhaps delving into the non-materialistic world, that place between mind, body, and spirit. In some cases, with the advancement of quantum physics, we already have done this. Now all we need to do is apply it to paranormal investigations.

Yet in the end, there's nothing better than plain old firsthand experience with the supernatural. And the Great Lakes region, to me, is a perfect place to start. I can recall some nights while staying in a cabin off Lake Superior in January, I would stay up late just gazing across the lake, watching and listening to the thunderous waves crashing against the shoreline. I also marveled at the ice sculptures naturally created from the water as it splashed the cliffs nearby. I often wondered what strange creatures lurked beneath the waves or along its coastline, what mysteries were slithering about just beyond the safety of the cabin lights. I would have liked to stay out there for hours, except for the fact that the temperature had to have been at least ten below.

As for ghostly apparitions, Dogman creatures, or phantom ladies in white, perhaps they are drawn to the water just as I am—mesmerized by the blue beauty of the lakes. They can't help but to be near the grand bodies of water, becoming an embodiment of both life and death.

Or maybe, like I indicated earlier, that they are using the lakes as a catalyst, able to more readily materialize into our world. Many paranormal experts believe that water acts like a conductor for the spirit world, allowing them to easily flow into our reality, and then back again to their own. Whether it's a ghostly spirit or a demon of the red devil type using portals, the water may certainly add to their power.

In the end, it's exciting to read the stories within this book, or other mysterious and spooky tales—especially around a campfire late at night. But if you're like me, you always wonder just how much truth is in them—which ultimately leads to the quintessential question when dealing with the paranormal: Do you believe? Do you see the events within these stories as fact or fiction? Do ghosts and devilish creatures really exist? Let me ask you another question: Have you ever seen something you cannot explain? If your answer is yes, then that, my friend, is an open invitation to the mysterious unknown—the world of the paranormal.

There's a constant theme in many of the books that I've written, where I ask, "Do you believe?" Of course, there's one simple way for you to find out. Take a trip to the other side of your reality. You don't have to travel too far—just make one little step and see what happens. Perhaps you start with a trip to the Great Lakes. Duluth, Minnesota; Mackinaw Island, Michigan; Detroit, Michigan; or maybe Niagara Falls—all these worlds are waiting for you. And maybe, just maybe, the supernatural world is waiting for you, too.

Ancient map showing the monsters of the sea—could there be the same such monsters of the Great Lakes?